MW01232150

The Kolokol Papers

THE
KOLOKOL
PAPERS

Larry Bograd

FARRAR · STRAUS · GIROUX
New York

Grateful acknowledgment is made to Macmillan Publishing
Co., Inc., for permission to use lines from "The Second
Coming," by William Butler Yeats, copyright 1924 by
Macmillan Publishing Co., Inc., copyright renewed 1952 by
Bertha Georgie Yeats

Library of Congress Cataloging in Publication Data
Bograd, Larry.
    The Kolokol papers.
    [1. Soviet Union—Fiction.   2. Dissenters—Fiction]
I. Title.
PZ7.B63579Ko   1981   [Fic]   81-15313
ISBN 0-374-34277-6   AACR2

Book design by Charlotte Staub

For my family—Ruth, Michele, and Harve—
with love, gratitude, and admiration

The Kolokol Papers

1

In the middle of the night, men came and took my father away in a big black car.

I heard the knock at the door, heard my father slowly descend the stairs, followed by my mother, heard the door open and the sound of voices, heard the footsteps of several men up the stairs, loud, over the protests of my parents.

Still I stayed in bed, my head turned away from the door, my heart pounding harder and harder as the commotion neared, my eyes open, my body sweaty, as I tried with full concentration to understand the voices in the hall.

The door to Grandma's room opened. She screamed, yelling at the men to stay away. The familiar creak of her

3

closet door was followed by the thud of her bed being pushed aside.

"Lev, I'm scared," my sister, Yulia, whispered to me.

"Shhh," I said, "be quiet."

I heard them sweep through the house: the sound of books being thrown from shelves; booted footsteps up and down the stairs; drawers being pulled, their contents dumped; glass breaking.

Then the oddest silence after the fury. I tried to calm my breathing, which was raspy and irregular, but couldn't.

"Where are they?" Yulia whispered.

"Shhh," I said. "They could still be here."

"Where are Mama and Papa?"

"Quiet," I said, wishing that I knew.

Then I heard the doorknob being turned. I had turned it so many times without ever noticing a sound, and now it creaked as if all its parts were rusted.

And I heard my mother shout, "Don't you dare go in there! Leave our children alone."

"I have my orders," a strange voice responded calmly.

As the door swung open, Yulia and I sat up in our beds. The silhouette of a man wearing a topcoat and hat was replaced by a blinding flashlight.

I shaded my eyes, trying to see who was there, but couldn't because of the bright light.

"I am Inspector Malatov. Give your names," a voice ordered.

I looked over at Yulia. She had pulled the covers up to the bridge of her nose.

"Your names," Malatov repeated.

"I am Lev Kolokol," I said.

"Yulia Kolokol," my sister said. She was crying.

The light flashed around our room from the doorway. Around the walls, the length of the ceiling, from our beds to the small desk and dresser we shared, back to our faces.

"Stay in bed and do not get up," Malatov told us.

4

The light moved out of our room, shifting down the hall. Framed in the doorway I saw our parents, barefoot, in their robes, uncombed hair, surrounded by Malatov and three men in uniforms.

The men and our parents moved down the stairs. As they left, Grandma came into our room, went to Yulia's bed, and hugged her.

"What is happening, Grandma?" I asked.

"Wait until they're gone," she said.

Outside the house a car started, and I looked out the window to see Father being forced into the back seat, a man in uniform on either side of him. Malatov stepped into the front seat and closed the door, and the car was off.

I followed its progress down our street until it disappeared around the corner.

Mama ran up the stairs and into our room. She came to my bed. Before I could react, she embraced me tightly. She seemed very calm. I don't know why, but this upset me.

"Irina . . ." Grandma started.

"They've arrested Sergei," Mother said. "Father has been taken away. That's all I know. Lev, Yulia, try to get some sleep. We will need our strength now more than ever."

"Mama, can I come sleep with you?" Yulia asked. "I'm scared." She started to cry again.

"Of course, dear, come with me. Lev, will you be all right?"

"Yes," I said, though I, too, didn't want to be alone.

That evening was the last time I saw Father in our home.

2

We waited fifteen months before seeing Father. During that time the authorities continually set back the date for his trial, never telling us the reason. We had no way of knowing if Father was alive, or if he had to recover from some torture inflicted upon him to make him confess. Perhaps the authorities were hoping the world would forget him, so they could quietly dispose of him.

After his arrest there were times I thought the whole thing was Father's idea; that he wasn't taken from us but, rather, left us. Had he assumed a new identity and moved away to be free of us? Was I such a terrible son that he'd go to such lengths just to be rid of me? Had the life of a dissident under the Soviets broken his spirit, sending him into flight?

He had often spoken of morality and conscience as being our duties, especially in a society that places so little honor on these qualities. But had he ever stopped to realize that he asked nothing less than a lifelong commitment against insurmountable odds? That he expected me to lead a life that the society I live in would look down upon, casting me aside as a "parasite" or "troublemaker"?

I saw Father for the last time at his trial, yet I didn't say goodbye to him; I refuse to. For better or worse, I will always be his son. He has only us to help him withstand this terrible time and he counts on us to be strong.

It is my duty to tell Father's story and, in doing this, tell my own and the story of this society. Like many duties, mine was neither chosen nor assigned; rather, it fell upon me, like a curse—or a blessing.

I must put everything down on paper, hoping an understanding will emerge. Until buried or understood, the past remains our present. There can be no changes until we accept what there is to know.

Now I must wait, as Father once did, for the big black car, for the knock at the door. Writing my story is a crime I may pay for with my life.

Downtown Moscow must look like a spider's web from high in the sky. The city radiates in concentric rings from a center made up by the symbols of the state: Red Square, the Kremlin, the Lenin Mausoleum.

Moscow is home: the only city I know, the only place I've ever been. Everything is familiar. The long lines outside food shops. People reading books to pass the wait. The smell of diesel oil. The wide streets and enormous squares. The drunks lying down in the underpasses. The parked automobiles without windshield wipers because

7

the owners have taken them inside to prevent theft. The simple, standard clothing covering the squat hordes of office workers. The rumble of trucks. Street vendors. Party posters. Motherland. People watching people; always the suspicion of being under surveillance. The "glory of the Socialist Revolution" and its machinery of state terror. The watchers and the watched.

Like that of most Russians, our family's Sunday amusement was a walk. If the weather was nice, the walk could last all afternoon.

I remember one Sunday when I was five or six years old, well before Yulia was born. It was a pleasant spring afternoon. What made it pleasanter still was that it marked the end of another long winter. Februaries are so cold one assumes growth will never return to the trees. They are as bare and gray as the winter sky.

But that day the first green buds of spring were on the trees. They appeared so suddenly it seemed as though they emerged overnight. Of course, they hadn't. It had taken most of the month of March for spring to arrive.

My father, Sergei Ivanovich Kolokol, walked ahead. He said a long walk was "therapeutic," a chance to stretch his mind as well as his legs. His pace was brisk, but he'd stop and look in store windows, giving us a chance to catch up. I walked between my mother, Irina, and Grandma, Father's mother. Grandma has lived with us as long as I can remember. She is my only living grandparent.

We turned down Gorky Street, and Father, as usual, began to teach. He extended one hand like an actor introducing a scene. "Gorky Street, Lev," he said, "one of Moscow's most important roads since it leads from the Kremlin. For centuries it was narrow and twisting, lined with old wooden houses. That is, until Stalin got hold of it. He destroyed its past, its character, and replaced it with the modern expanse we now see—full of traffic and ex-

8

pensive shops for foreigners." He dropped his hand to his side. "So much for the Great Five-Year Plan."

We stopped at the Central Post Office so Father could mail a letter. Inside the building was a large illuminated, spinning globe. I always loved this globe: a planet revolving freely in the U.S.S.R.

Farther down Gorky Street, we stopped in Soviet Square. An imposing building stands at the back of the square, the Party Archives of the Institute of Marxism-Leninism.

Across the square is another monument, an equestrian statue of Prince Dolgoruky, the founder of Moscow. It was erected in 1954 in honor of the eight hundredth anniversary of the city. Eight hundred years of history, of regimes strong and weak, of revolutions and counterrevolutions, of death and repression, of art and glory. Moscow has held much.

The Soviets have done their best to make Moscow their own after less than seventy years of control. Streets were renamed to honor Soviet heroes. Old statues were replaced by ones of the leaders of the October Revolution.

I suppose every government rewrites history to fit its purposes; the compromise of the past is only more obvious here.

Another sure sign of spring was the food vendors on the square. Father stopped to buy everyone a glass of sweet water. An American I once met with my father compared this drink with very watery lemonade.

Father paid the vendor and left him a tip. Then he turned from the vendor's pushcart with his glass. He clinked it against each of ours and toasted our health.

Then he raised the glass as if to salute the two KGB agents who had followed us since we left home.

They did not react. Father shook his head and smiled.

"Come," he said, having finished his drink. "Let's head home. We don't want to keep our 'friends' out all day.

The sun is not good for their type. And they must have families they'd rather be with on such a nice afternoon."

We returned the glasses to the vendor, who quickly wiped them off and turned them down on a tray.

Mother walked with Father in front. Grandma took my hand and we strolled behind. Occasionally I looked back at the two agents, who were smoking cigarettes. I had come to recognize their appearance: black coats and trousers, white shirts, thin black ties, solemn faces.

"Grandma, why do those men always follow us?"

"Those men are the lowest creatures on earth," she said. "They have no decency."

"But why us? Why do they watch us?"

"They watch many people," she said. "Your parents are important people because they have free minds. And because they are free, they are a threat to the Soviets. They want everyone to act one way and always be afraid of freedom. But we're not scared, are we, dear?"

"I'm not!"

"That's my handsome grandson," she said, squeezing my hand.

At that age I didn't really view the agents as "instruments of the state" any more than I understood my family were "enemies of the state." Then the world was divided into two camps: grown-ups and children. Grownups were big people with all the answers. And, for us children, our world was the one they provided. They gave us a way to see the world, told us the difference between right and wrong, charted our attitudes, cemented our likes and dislikes.

I knew only that my parents were right, that their friends were good people I should hug and tell stories to, that they were involved in important work—though it was impossible for me to know just how serious human-rights activities were. Like many other lessons, the realization of my parents' "specialness" would come with my own growing up.

When I was old enough to start school, outfoxing the KGB was still a game. I remember finding an old accordion in the closet. It had belonged to my mother's family; an uncle had given it to her years before. I never learned to play it well, but my parents kept requesting I get the instrument out and bang on it. I was certain they thought I had talent.

Years later they confessed I played terribly. They just needed a noise cover to talk under, since our apartment was bugged. "Forgive me, Lev," Father said, "but if your accordion playing gave the KGB the same headaches it gave me and your mother over the years, I'll be very happy!"

Turning on the radio loud to cover any important conversation was a way of life for us. In fact, I thought it was a law: one must have noisy music before speaking.

Toys and games are now left to Yulia, though even she will one day understand how serious life is for us. My parents and their friends have always tried to shelter her—as they tried to shelter me—but in the Soviet Union one can remain sequestered in childhood's innocence for only a limited term.

11

3

$\mathbf{M}$y family has been followed for as long as I can remember. But as a child I didn't realize I was also being watched. I knew my parents and their friends were doing something special, and I now realize that in the authorities' eyes I was one of them.

Everyone wants to believe his or her family is special as well as the model of normality, that if a family is well known it is for socially admirable reasons. It wasn't until I entered school that I came to understand that my family was considered out-of-step and dangerous.

Certain episodes became focal points of my awareness of how different my family was. One such episode was that springtime walk, another occurred at the end of my first year of school.

In the Soviet Union we start school at the age of seven. The Soviets like to point out that by the age of eight Russian children read as well as eleven-year-old Americans. While most American children spend years using readers with controlled vocabularies, we are introduced to our literary heritage as soon as we master the alphabet. Our first-grade *bukvar*, or reader, had "Little Philip," a fairy tale by Tolstoy; poems by Pushkin and Lermontov, and a fable by Krylov.

Along with pre-Soviet authors, we receive our first Soviet indoctrination in first grade. There was a section in my *bukvar* called "In Lenin's Day." We read how Lenin loved children, how he visited an orphanage and played games. I remember the full-page picture of a smiling Lenin sitting on a park bench, his arm around a little girl as he listened to a boy reciting from a book. He seemed friendly, a sweet, thoughtful man. Russian children grow up accepting Lenin as the lovable father of our collective family.

I arrived home from school a few days before my eighth birthday, wearing the standard school uniform: long gray trousers, gray tunic with a leather belt, and a peaked cap. (The girls wear dark brown dresses with little white collars and over the dresses black pinafores.) "Guess what I learned today at school?" I asked my parents.

"What, Lev dear?" Mother responded.

"The pledge of the Octobrists," I said. I stood up straight and recited, "I, a young Octobrist of the Soviet Union, promise in the presence of my comrades to love my Soviet fatherland, to live and strive as our great Lenin showed us, as the Communist Party teaches us."

My parents and grandmother were horrified.

"Oh, my God," Grandma said, holding her head.

"Everyone in my class gets to join," I told them. "They're going to give us neckerchiefs!"

The Octobrists are, of course, named after the October Revolution of 1917, which brought the Soviets to power.

I couldn't understand why my parents weren't happy. Didn't they want me to participate in the school clubs? I was sure it'd be fun: marching and learning songs, going on field trips. I didn't want to be left out.

"Come on, dinner is ready," Mother said. "We'll discuss this later."

"Irina . . ." Father started to say.

"Hush," she said. "We'll eat first. We should have expected this, Sergei Ivanovich. He's only a child."

"But he's *our* child," Father said.

I had no idea what I had done wrong. Joining the Octobrists was something that was expected at school, the first step in becoming a good citizen. No one talked during dinner. Father chewed slowly, tapping his fork on the plate's edge. The mucus building up in my throat made it impossible to swallow. I didn't touch the kasha, usually my favorite dish.

After dinner, when Grandma went into the kitchen to do the dishes, my parents sat me down in my room and turned on the radio.

"Lev darling," Mother started softly, sitting down next to me. Her weight on the mattress caused me to lean against her. "We hope you will understand what we want to say. It may be difficult. But your father and I have had to make some important decisions that will affect you."

I'd never seen them like this: calm, yet upset with me. I wanted some anger, some shouting—something I could deal with and react to. Instead, they only looked sad. I now realize they were not so much disappointed as aware that they could no longer keep something terrible away from me. I could no longer be protected.

"People here are not free to share ideas and information," Father said, sitting across from me. "The state does not want us to think and speak for ourselves. The Soviets tell us who can work, and where. They tell us what we can

14

know. They don't want us to make up our own minds. And they're willing to use force—and have, repeatedly—to keep us from acting as free people. They say anyone who speaks against them hates our country. This isn't so. Your mother and I love Russia, but have decided we have to do more to let the world know about the situation here."

"You remember Georgy Yakir?" Mother asked.

"Yes," I said, though at that time I knew him only as my friend Tanya's father. And that he was in jail.

"When Georgy was arrested and sent away, we worked to get him released," Mother continued. "To do this, we had to talk to lots of people and send lots of letters. And the Soviets didn't like this. They wished we'd just forget Georgy. But we never did. He's our friend, and the people one loves are more important than how some strangers may tell you to act."

"What does this have to do with the Octobrists?" I asked. "Everyone at school is joining. It's just a club. I want to go to camp with my friends. Please. Can't I?" Like all children that age, I knew that I had no recourse but to follow my parents' wishes. Still, did I have to be punished and made an outsider at school?

"The Octobrists are a Party organization," Father said. "It's part of the system, like the KGB men who always follow us. It's a bad thing, son. The Octobrists are only the first step to adjust you to the Soviet system. It's the first time they can start to shape your mind to think only one way—the way they want you to."

"No they don't," I said. "Alexis told me all about it. His brother belongs. They sing songs and march and play games. They go special places to see things. And have fun."

I remember Father leaning back and talking to Mother as if I weren't in the room. "Irina, it's no use. The boy's too young. I think we'll have to make the decision for him."

15

"But that's not fair," I shouted. "Why can you tell me what to do?"

"Lev, can you understand this is how the system works? We want you to have friends and go places and have fun. But we don't believe the Octobrists are a good thing. Do you want someone acting like parents your whole life, always telling you what to do? By not joining, you'll be your own person and will show everyone you can make up your own mind. Wouldn't you rather do that?"

I said, "I guess so." But I really didn't.

From that day on, a tightrope was set. At school I would be expected to act one way, the proper Soviet way. At home I'd become the son of the Kolokols, who opposed the Soviet system with all their energies.

For nearly the past ten years, I have been caught in the middle, until now deciding to write my own story. It *is* better to face the consequences of being a free person, even if that freedom may one day be spent in a prison camp. I'm sure my parents must have also faced this dilemma, though it is easy to forget at times that they had their own lives growing up.

We had a family scrapbook—now taken away by the authorities—which I used to take down and leaf through. There I saw my parents as I never actually knew them. How different they looked when they were younger, yet I could always pick them out from a group. There was an essence in the face, in the way the body was held, that always indicated my parents to me.

Father standing stiffly in the front row of his class. His hair, then dark and thick, parted slickly down the middle. Unlike me, Father knew what he wanted to do with his life. He trained to be a mathematician, and was until the authorities took away his academic certification and his career. His family was prosperous, as my grandfather was chief surgeon at a large hospital. But then came Grand-father's arrest and internal exile.

Father, in his first year of college, started his political involvement by trying to find out his father's fate. It was his first lesson on how the system works.

From the photographs taken during summer vacations in the Crimea, it was easy to see why Father had a reputation as an athlete. He was always strong, as I learned from our occasional wrestling sessions, though he became a little overweight. He had trouble keeping his trousers from slipping below his potbelly.

Mother, in her school pictures, was serious, too. It was easy to find her, since her eyes had not changed over the years. They were dark and deep and met yours straight on. In every photograph she seemed to be looking through the camera, trying to make contact with the photographer.

Mother has always kept her hair long. In the photographs it was worn braided on top of her head. The last time I saw her, her hair was streaked with gray and pulled back, clasped at the nape of her neck.

She had beautiful hands. Unlike Father's, which were thick-fingered, almost pawlike, Mother's hands had long and graceful fingers.

She wanted to be a pianist and must have been talented, since she was accepted as a student at the conservatory. While in school she studied English as well as music. I've had English since primary school and, on occasion, had to come to Mother's aid when she couldn't think of the proper word.

Mother had to withdraw from the conservatory after she married Father. Even then he was marked as a trou-blemaker and had difficulty securing a teaching position. So her wonderfully graceful fingers never touched a piano again. Instead, she used them to work in a tailor shop as a seamstress, doing more sewing late into the night to

17

bring in a little extra money. Sometimes she'd exchange a sewing job for a favor, perhaps getting a ream of paper or some fresh fruit in return.

When Father lost his teaching job he began to spend his time researching and writing a detailed history of human-rights violations within the U.S.S.R. He hoped, when it was released, that the document would force the Soviets to adhere to international agreements they had signed—but never put into practice: allowing freedom of travel, freedom from religious persecution, and the free dissemination of information. When she came home and didn't have her own work to do, Mother helped Father with his manuscript.

I used to dream of the day when we could have a piano in our home so I could hear how Mother played. But that day never came.

4

By the time I started high school, even before Father's arrest, I had fewer and fewer friends. I was no longer a comrade, I was the son of Sergei and Irina Kolokol. I was the son, not of Sergei Kolokol the mathematician, but of Sergei Kolokol the dissident. My mother was not merely a seamstress, but Irina Kolokol, the wife of Sergei Ivanovich and an activist in her own right.

It became a family joke that I had no calling for mathematics. I suspect Father was disappointed, but he never said anything. I had done well with math until we reached advanced geometry. Then, for some reason, I just couldn't keep all the shapes straight in my mind. And whenever

I asked someone at school to help, I received the same answer, "Sorry, I'm too busy."

Math wasn't the only thing my classmates used to isolate me. Whenever they could, they let me know I didn't belong.

"Want to sit with me during lunch?" I asked Andrey, one of my classmates.

"No," he answered, "I already promised Liza."

"How about playing some basketball after school?" I asked Dmitri.

"Sorry, Kolokol, but we're forming a team for the school league and the roster is already full," he said.

"Listen, I know I'm not the best player, but I'm no worse than most of the guys," I said. "Please let me play."

"Sorry," Dmitri said. He shrugged his shoulders and walked away.

"Do you want to work together on the history project?" I asked Marya. "I have most of it done already, so there wouldn't be too much work left."

"No, thank you," she said. "I'd better not."

"Why not?" I asked.

"Oh, just because. I have to go—don't want to be late for my next class. 'Bye." She lifted her books to her chest and turned away.

And so it went as my parents became more notorious as dissidents. Just when I thought I'd spend my high-school days in total isolation, along came Peter Simonov to become my friend.

In retrospect, I suppose I should have been suspicious of Peter's intentions all along. He came from a proper Soviet family. His father was well connected and his family had prospered because of it. Yet when I was with Peter I never had the feeling that he was watching me, ready to report anything he found out to the authorities. I thought he was my friend. Of course, I never told him anything very important—it wasn't that type of friendship. It was companionship, something no one else at school had extended to me.

Although Peter and I had gone to school for years we hadn't known each other that well. Instead of hanging around after class, Peter would pick up his slide rule, piles of notebooks, and college textbooks taken from the science library, and go home to work in the chemistry lab his father had put in their apartment. Peter hated athletics. "Sports are for mindless barbarians who can't control their violent urges," he'd say. "The only true games are games of the mind, like chess or mathematical puzzles. These are the real tests of a person's worth." Then he'd push his eyeglasses back into place and look at you as if you were an idiot.

Our friendship began the day Peter asked me to join him after school in his laboratory.

The Simonovs had a big apartment in a new building. While we had three tiny bedrooms, a living room, and a kitchen, the Simonovs had five large bedrooms, a den, a dining room, two bathrooms, a kitchen twice the size of ours, and Peter's laboratory. Their apartment had big windows and plenty of light, and a covered terrace. The walls were clean and white, the shelves full of plants and pottery. The living room was dominated by a large portrait of Lenin.

"How long have you been interested in chemistry?" I asked Peter.

"Quite a long time now," he said. "I memorized the periodic table of the elements when I was five years old. When I recited them in order, giving their electron configurations and atomic weights, my father gave me my first lab set."

We spent an hour doing various projects in the lab. Peter showed me how to mix several chemicals together to glow in the dark. We powered a toy boat across the sink by dropping a little vinegar onto baking soda.

"Seems like you can do anything in this lab."

"Almost," Peter said, jotting down some reaction formulas. "I can even make explosives."

"Why would you want to make explosives?" I asked.

"Oh, I don't know. It's fun to watch things blow up. Why don't I write down the formula for making gunpowder and you take it home and study it. Maybe we can even mix up a batch sometime."

"Okay," I said. "Listen, I have to meet Tanya Yakir at her gymnastics class. Want to come with me?"

"Tanya Yakir? Isn't she the daughter of Georgy Yakir?" Peter asked.

"Yes, how did you know?"

"Oh well, I suppose I heard her name mentioned someplace. I don't remember right off where," he said. "After all, her father . . . have you known her long?"

"Just about my whole life," I answered. "Our parents are good friends."

"But they're Jews, aren't they?"

"Yes, they're Jewish. What of it?" I asked.

"Oh, nothing," Peter said, closing his notebook. "Here is the explosive formula. I think it's pretty straightforward."

I looked it over and had no idea what was written down. I was bothered by Peter's comments about the Yakirs. "You don't have anything against Jews, do you?"

"Of course not," he said. "My family has done business in their shops for years. I just can't understand why those people make such a stink about leaving our country to go to a place like Israel which is merely a puppet for capitalist imperialist warmongers. That's all."

"Well, under recent international agreement, they have a right to leave, don't they?"

"Of course. They can leave at any time as far as I'm

concerned," he said. "I don't understand why they'd want to, that's all."

"Let's go," I said. "I don't want to keep Tanya waiting."

Georgy Yakir and my parents had attended the university at the same time, though while my Father studied mathematics and my mother literature and music, Georgy was in the philosophy department.

When Georgy was arrested in Pushkin Square in January of 1967, my parents—among many others—could remain silent no longer. He was there protesting the arrest of four citizens charged with "anti-Soviet agitation and propoganda." There were more KGB agents than demonstrators in the crowd, so Georgy was arrested and sentenced to a seven-year prison camp term.

Tanya was two years old when Georgy entered prison. She was nine on his release, and Georgy cried when he saw her since he had brought home a simple wooden toy he quickly realized Tanya was too old to still be playing with.

"Are you getting ready for the Olympics?" Peter asked Tanya when she took a break from the balance beam.

"Yes," she said. "One day I shall represent the state of Israel." Tanya could be very serious, even when the situation did not call for it.

"Israel?" Peter asked. "Why not represent our country?"

"Your country, perhaps," she said, wiping her forehead with a towel, "but when the government lets us emigrate —as is our legal right—Israel will be my country."

"Whatever you say." Peter did not want to create a scene.

"Hurry up and shower. We'll wait outside," I said. "Let's go get some tea and cake."

Because she attended a different school, I rarely saw Tanya. Our parents were good friends, and I had a feeling they thought Tanya and I might marry someday. Not that I was against the idea. Whenever our families got together,

I tried to find some time to be alone with Tanya. It wasn't easy.

Tanya looked athletic—I liked that. She was tall, had long, frizzy red hair that she kept in pigtails, and freckles that I once tried to count but lost track of before crossing her nose. When she looked at me with her green eyes, I knew she really liked me. She never exactly came out and said as much, but then, neither did I.

Peter was my everyday friend, but Tanya was special. Our friendship was bonded through our parents' long association. Like my father, her father had been kicked out of the Academic Union, since he did not go along with the edict to restrict free speech. My parents and the Yakirs had been active in the democratic movement for all the years Tanya and I were growing up. Often I was left at her home—or vice versa—when our parents went to meetings.

The stop at the café was far from pleasant. Tanya didn't even pretend to be friendly, though Peter made every effort to be nice. I was caught in the middle, trying to find things the three of us could talk about calmly. I had hoped they'd get along since both were my friends. I should have known better.

"How can you want to be a chemist," Tanya asked Peter, "when you'd be denied access to information from around the world, information which could benefit you? How will you feel doing research in an intellectual vacuum?"

"Considering our scientists lead the world in innovation, I don't foresee being denied anything," he responded.

"What makes you think that's the truth? The Soviets live by lies. All they need are citizens selfish enough to close their eyes to their ways."

"Tanya, keep your voice down," I asked. "You're attracting attention."

"Don't tell me what to do, Lev Kolokol," she shouted.

24

"You may be afraid of informants, but I'm not. They have already done everything they could to break my father's spirit, and we are still here fighting for our rights. They can take everything away from you if you wish, but I won't let them. I'm proud to be a free-thinking Jew. They will never break my faith." She was gripping her tea glass so tightly I was waiting for it to shatter.

"Are you going to the track meet next weekend?" I asked Peter, changing the subject.

"Of course," he said, "and I wouldn't be surprised to see some world records broken."

"That's because Soviet athletes are shot full of steroids," Tanya said. "It's sickening when a society will spend so much attention and money on athletics when so many people are suffering."

"You're a gymnast"—Peter gestured toward Tanya—"you should talk."

"Listen, Peter Simonov, I will never wear the Soviet uniform as long as I live. I compete now for myself, and one day for my people." She looked at me coldly, as if somehow I was at fault for Peter's attitudes.

Peter made a pretense of looking at his watch. "I really should be going. Lev, I'll see you in the morning." He stood up and looked across the table. "And good day to you, Tanya Yakir. I hope the next time I find you in better spirits."

"There's nothing wrong with my spirits that decent company wouldn't improve."

Peter walked off one way, Tanya and I the other. I tried to take her hand, but she moved away, crossing her arms over her chest.

"I can't believe you've allowed Peter Simonov to become your friend," she said.

"Why not? There's nothing wrong with him," I said. "Besides, I'd never tell him anything important. He's just a chum."

"Aren't you the least bit suspicious that now is the time he decides to be your friend?"

"Tanya, no one at school will as much as talk to me!"

"Do you think it's any different for me?" She stopped, forcing me to look at her. "His father is an official with the Academic Union. Peter has never taken a side step in his life. I just know he's been assigned to follow you, to get you into trouble somehow."

"Come on!" I said and started to walk off. I couldn't believe what she was suggesting. Was she jealous of Peter, was that it? "You're saying that the authorities have nothing better to do than have a teenager followed and kept track of, is that it?"

"That's precisely what I'm saying," she said. "Who knows what you may tell Peter once he has your confidence. You may betray our parents and the movement without ever knowing it. The authorities can take the most innocent statement or action and blow it into a scandal. People have been sent away millions of times just because the state did not want them around. I should know, shouldn't I?"

"You're being too sensitive, Tanya Yakir, and don't underestimate me." I walked back and took her in my arms. She did not resist, although her body was stiff and she kept her arms by her sides.

She looked straight into my eyes, alternating her stare from my left eye to my right and back again. "Lev, you must realize what one free person means to them—it's a threat to their whole system. Their whole existence depends solely on control. Repression is their passion . . . Lev, be careful with Peter Simonov. He is not to be trusted."

"Who is?"

"In this society, so few." She reached up, placing her hands behind my neck. I kissed her several times, but she

26

did not respond. "You and I—we didn't ask for our lives," she said quietly. "We have to be careful or we will certainly lose what little we're allowed to have."

At the time my only thought, I remember, was wishing events would prove her fears wrong.

5

I walked Tanya home, stopping in to see Anna, her mother, and Natasha, her one-year-old sister. Georgy was still at the museum where he worked as a maintenance man.

Anna sat on the couch, her blouse raised so Natasha could nurse. I felt a little embarrassed being there, but Anna made no pretense. Babies must nurse.

"Your mother stopped by earlier this afternoon," Anna said.

"For what?"

"She brought us a chicken, which was so thoughtful. She gave the woman at the shop a blouse she had sewn in exchange for the meat. And she brought some wonder-

28

ful news. Your parents received . . ." She stood up, cradling Natasha, and turned on the radio, then she returned to the couch. "Your parents received a message from Simon Reese, their contact at the American Embassy. He has a copy of a telegram sent to the Kremlin from the President!"

I was always the last to hear such news. "What did it say?"

"No one knows," Anna said, adjusting Natasha in her arm. "Simon Reese will send the telegram to your parents by a journalist friend of his. Can I get you a cup of tea, Lev?"

"No, thank you. I'd better get going."

Tanya came in, having put on a sweater. "When will I see you again?" she asked me.

"Soon, I hope. Maybe Sunday we can go for a walk."

"Until then," she said and gave me a kiss on the cheek.

It was freezing walking home. The snow was crusty, tinted blue. The dusk air was thick and pink, with flecks of ice sparkling in it. Under my boots the snow crunched noisily.

The shops on my route were more crowded than usual —no doubt due to the cold. People went in not to buy but to thaw out, to wipe cold tears from their eyes and stamp their feet. I would've joined them if I'd had much farther to go.

Walking as fast as I could, my hands deep in the pockets of my overcoat, I reached my street and ran the last block home.

Across the street I saw two agents standing in the doorway. When I opened the door to our building, our downstairs neighbor cracked her door to see who had entered.

"Good day to you, Katherina," I said.

She shut her door without saying a word.

Upstairs in our apartment there were a few reporters, and the radio was on loud.

I went over and kissed Mother. "What's all this about?" I whispered. "Anna told me about the telegram."

"We'll talk later. You look frozen. Go to the kitchen and put the water on for tea."

It was not unusual to see foreign journalists in our apartment. Father had become one of the leading dissidents, since most of the better-known activists either had been forced to emigrate or were in internal exile. In the past year my parents had moved to the forefront of the movement, our home becoming the base where supporters from the West dropped off goods or money smuggled in for the families of dissidents who had been silenced.

The people from the West who came to our home were always concerned about our well-being, even though they were risking their own by visiting us. Without their help, we'd have been dangerously isolated from the rest of the world.

No matter where they came from, all foreigners were told the same joke on their first visit to our apartment.

"What nationality were Adam and Eve?" Father would ask with a grin.

"I don't know. What?"

"Adam and Eve were Russian," Father would reply.

"I don't get it," was the usual response.

Father would explain: "Because they didn't have any clothes, had only an apple to eat—and were told they were living in Paradise."

There was a new face at the meeting. He had to be an American, with his long hair, mustache, and very expensive clothes. He wore a beautiful wool suit that fitted him perfectly, a checked shirt, a thin brown tie, and cowboy boots!

The new American and the other reporters had their

notebooks out as Mother translated for Father, telling them of the expected message from the embassy.

After twenty minutes, it was over. Everyone had left but the American.

He stayed on the couch, smoking a cigarette, while I helped Mother clear the room of cups and glasses. When we had finished, he stood up, adjusted his tie, and stepped toward me.

"Percy Elliman," he said, extending his hand.

"Hello," I said, taking it. He gripped my hand and pumped it up and down.

We stood there awkwardly. I didn't know where to start, and apparently neither did he. He hadn't asked any questions during the meeting, although he attentively took notes.

Finally Mother asked, "Can we help you, Mr. Elliman?"

He reached into a leather bag, taking out cartons of American cigarettes and a large tin of baked ham. "These are for you," he said, handing them to Mother. "Simon Reese is my friend. We went to college together. He gave me something else to give to you." He reached inside his jacket and handed Mother an envelope. "I hope it was okay to wait until the others left before I gave you the message. Simon told me the KGB often have foreign journalists in their control."

"You did the right thing, Mr. Elliman. I want to show it to my husband," Mother said. "Thank you for the cigarettes and ham. And welcome to Moscow. Do you plan to stay long?"

"No, just for a couple of months. I received official credentials to do an article on Moscow's subway system, but I'm really here because I believe in what you people are doing."

"Well, thank you, Mr. Elliman. I must get my family's supper ready. Can you wait a moment to talk to my husband?"

"Yes."

Mother went into the kitchen, where Father had already begun preparing our meal.

Percy looked around the apartment. "Not much room here, is there?" he said with a smile.

"No," I said.

"Simon told me about you. Your name is Lev, right?"

I nodded. "Yes."

"I brought something for you as well." He reached into his leather bag and handed me a flat square wrapped in brown paper. "Go ahead, open it."

I tore the paper away to find a rock-and-roll record. "This is for me?"

"You have a stereo, don't you?"

"A stereo? No. We have an old phonograph with one small speaker."

"Well, as long as you have something you can play it on," he said with a grin.

"Thank you, Mr. Elliman."

"All my friends call me Percy. You should too."

Father came out of the kitchen, the telegram that Percy had delivered in his hand, and told me to thank Percy for him.

"Thank you for delivering this," I said to Percy.

"What does it say?" I asked Father.

"Not much," Father said. "Mother translated it for me. The President expresses his hope that the authorities will respect what he calls 'advocates of the freedom of the human spirit' and mentions my name as one person he admires. He lets the Kremlin know that he'll take into account how we are treated when he sits down and discusses trade or other important issues with the Soviet leadership. Ask Mr. Elliman what he thinks of the message."

Percy listened to my English, nodding that he understood.

"The diplomats call this 'linkage,' " Percy explained. "In other words, the White House is saying that the Soviets cannot expect to receive favorable treatment if they continue to repress human-rights activities. I hope the President's sincere, though I suspect he issued the statement for political reasons. You see, he wants to show the Kremlin—and the American voters—that he will take a hard line in his relations with the Soviets. But it's really too early to know if he'll back up his statement when the time for action comes."

I explained what Percy said, and Father asked me to tell him that we hoped to see him in our home again, and to thank him for his kindness.

"You're welcome," Percy said, picking up his leather bag. "If there's anything I can do . . ."

"Thank you," Father said, shaking Percy's hand.

Within forty-eight hours, the contents of the President's cable had been copied, using the old typewriter in our apartment. The typewriter was registered to a friend of my parents who still belonged to the Writers' Union. Using carbon paper and thin onionskin paper, Mother made dozens of copies, which were passed from hand to hand throughout the dissident community.

Certain dissidents were skeptical of the cable. "Just wait," Mochol Pevrod said. "The American opinion makers will question why the President would involve himself with human rights at a time when increased tension between the U.S.A. and the Soviets seems much more important. It will end up doing us no good."

Mochol Pevrod called herself a realist, though Mother, who was her friend, labeled her a pessimist. Mochol always expected the worst to happen—which it often did.

She had an important role in the movement—she knew how to get things done. Very few people knew of Mochol's work, and this served a purpose: she would not be an early target if and when the KGB cracked down on my parents and their associates. Mochol had many contacts: one person for supplying paper, another who had equipment for making microfilm. She had friends at the Western embassies who could arrange visas. Without her, my parents' work would have been much more difficult.

Father took the cable from his pocket and waved it at Mochol. "This is real, my friend," he said. "No one can deny it."

She nodded her head and sighed. "Sergei Ivanovich, for all our sakes I hope you're right."

6

For a change there was cause for celebration.

"Who cares if we're just a pawn in the Americans' geopolitics," Father said. "I hope the President's message sends shivers down the Politburo's hard old spines!"

So my parents hosted a gathering to celebrate. The living room was full of familiar faces from the dissident community. There were teachers no longer allowed to teach, doctors who could not attend their patients, poets whose poems were read only by their family and friends, musicians who now played for their own pleasure, no longer licensed for the public. But everyone was in a good mood. The night was for fun, not politics.

Tanya arrived with her father, Georgy. Anna stayed home with Natasha.

Georgy was a big bear of a man who had kisses for everyone. He kissed Mother twice, Yulia three times, Father four times, and Grandma six times. There was no stopping him. Tanya stood by, laughing at her father's clowning.

"You're next, Lev my boy!" Georgy shouted going after me. I got the table between us, but it was no use. He grabbed the back of my neck and pulled me forward, toppling me over. Holding my head in his hands, he kissed me on the lips six times.

Then Malsa Isakov arrived. She was embarrassed when Mother greeted her with a kiss. I didn't know why then; there were kisses everywhere.

Since the time she was Father's student, Malsa had become part of our family, though I never thought of her as a sister. I must confess, I had a terrible crush on her, often fantasizing about her.

Some evenings she came over when my parents weren't home and she'd sit with us until they returned. Finding some music on the radio, she'd get up to dance—which was always exciting to watch. Closing her hazel-colored eyes, she'd pull her long auburn hair from its clasp and shake it loose.

While Grandma would get up and go into another room, I'd get up and move my feet, attempting to dance. I'd shuffle my legs, jerk my arms up and down. Malsa, on the other hand, looked so natural in motion, her shoulders rolling, hips rotating, head moving from side to side.

Soon the party was in full swing with everyone crowded around the table. There were as many vodka and cognac bottles as people. The plates were attacked as if people hadn't eaten in months. There were herring, chicken, tomatoes, cucumbers with dill, and loaves of black bread.

And there was no age barrier. Parents brought their children. Grandparents, uncles, aunts, cousins—whoever could get there came.

That afternoon it seemed there was enough food to last an army for a week. But everything was gone by ten o'clock. Neighbors went home for additional supplies.

With the table and couch pushed back, the living room was cleared for dancing. Eased by vodka, no one was shy about how they danced or with whom.

There were fox-trots and mazurkas to old records. When someone found folk music among my parents' records, the evening became livelier still.

Georgy challenged Father to a dancing contest. Squatting and kicking their legs out to the music's beat, trying to balance empty bottles on their heads, Father and Georgy soon collapsed into each other's arms, laughing, crying, planting wet kisses on each other's cheek. Everyone applauded.

Late into the night, the less familiar faces had left, leaving only my parents' closest friends. Father was on the couch, between Mother and Malsa. They were talking politics, intent on rehashing arguments I had heard time and time again.

The radio was on loud and I had had enough noise for one evening. Walking into the kitchen, I found Tanya washing dishes at the sink. She was humming to herself and did not notice me. I snuck up and hugged her from behind. I hoped she'd be pleased; instead, she nearly dropped a dish.

"Lev, you shouldn't," she said, slapping my shoulder. "You scared me."

"I was trying to be nice."

"Nice?" Then her scowl melted into a grin. "Anyway, not here, not in the kitchen. They'll hear us," she said, pointing a soapy hand toward the living room.

"They're busy talking," I assured her. "Let's go into the hallway. They won't miss us." I took a towel and dried her hands. She moved closer and watched as if I were doing something strange. I leaned forward and kissed her cheek.

She leaned her head back. "Have you been drinking?"

"Just a little. Everyone has." I took her hand and led her from the sink. We quickly walked out of the kitchen and to the front door. No one seemed to notice.

We went down the hallway to a dark spot under a burned-out light bulb. She leaned against the wall, facing me. I quickly put my arms around her waist and started to kiss her.

She tilted her head to reach my lips. I moved my hands up the front of her blouse to her breasts. She didn't do anything except rub the back of my neck. How naturally the kisses came, one compelling the next to follow.

It took what seemed like an hour to unbutton the top two buttons of her blouse. Finally I slipped my hand inside. My fingers crept downward from her neck until they encountered her brassiere.

I opened my eyes to look at her, hoping for a signal, but her eyes were shut. Raising my elbow near her ear, I pushed my fingers under the elastic to feel the gentle slope of her breast. Her skin was so soft, so much smoother than anything I had ever felt on my own body.

She shifted her position, forcing my hand back. I was content to kiss a little longer before trying something else. Waiting long enough, I then dropped my other hand from her shoulder to her hips to see how she would react. She moved closer. Our chests were touching. Her hands were running up and down my back.

My hand traveled from her hip to her belly. She moved back a little to allow me to wedge my hand just inside the waist of her skirt. Her flesh against my palm, my fingers felt the band of her underwear. For me, this was all previously uncharted territory.

"Lev, please," she whispered softly between kisses.

I stopped for a moment but did not retreat.

"Please, Lev, please."

I thought for certain she was asking me to go on, wanting me.

She pushed her hips into mine. I forced my fingers farther down. Her hands were on my shoulders as if she was preventing me from lifting off the ground.

"Please," she said, moving her head away. "No, Lev, stop it!"

"Stop it?" I couldn't believe it. "Why?"

She looked into my eyes. I didn't know what to say, what she wanted to hear. Was there something specific to say that would allow me to go on? She shook her head, reached down to lift my hand up and away. And then, without a word, she turned from me and walked down the hall and back into the apartment.

Why was she doing this to me?

I waited a couple of minutes before going back inside, trying to calm down.

Apparently I was not missed, for no one noticed when I returned; they were too busy talking.

Tanya was seated on the couch next to Georgy. I was so mad at her I couldn't look at anyone else. If she wasn't interested, why did she go into the hallway with me? What did she think we were going to do, organize youth against Soviet tyranny? She stared at me briefly before leaning against her father's shoulder.

"Why can't the people expect no censorship, the truthful reporting of events, and respect for a citizen's right to free speech?" Georgy said.

"Don't ask me." Father shrugged. "Ask the Kremlin."

"What we must accept for the present is that the

regime is still prepared and able to use repression and scare tactics to prevent the spread of the democratic movement," Mother said, as if she were repeating the point for the millionth time. "People know the Soviets will do anything to maintain their power. Still, it is apathy here and in the West that is our worst enemy."

For several minutes there was silence.

I was getting uncomfortable looking at the thoughtful adults. Had they run out of talk? I had never thought it possible. Was their spirit broken? This, too, was impossible. But they sat as if terrible news had arrived and thrown the household into shocked silence.

Finally Georgy looked up, opened up his hands palm up as if pleading, and asked, "So where lies our hope? Tell me that."

Mother said, "Look forward to Lev's and Tanya's grandchildren perhaps living in a free society, but not before. For the present the government is not open to reform. It is tuned for repression, not for listening to its citizens' grievances."

"So why continue the struggle?" someone then asked.

"Because it is the only thing honorable people can do," Father replied. "That we are here is important far beyond the walls of the Kremlin. There must be people who will surrender to neither apathy nor terror if there is to be hope and a sense of the future."

The evening ended, as such evenings usually did, with hugs of reassurance. All had spoken their minds, unloaded their frustrations, reinforced the strength of their friendship.

Tanya had clung to Georgy the rest of the evening. But as she left, she gave me a look which I think meant I was forgiven. I had nothing to say to her. I felt bad about upsetting her but was angry that she had made me feel like some foolish ogre. Still, I was glad she left not hating me.

I went to bed, my head light from vodka, my thoughts full of food and faces and words and blaring music.

7
══════════

The telegram from the American President continued to be a catalyst of hope for the dissident community. Protests grew bolder. Several people were arrested after unfolding a banner demanding the freeing of political prisoners. More and more journalists interviewed my parents. The atmosphere was charged; more illegal articles were circulated among our friends. New faces started to attend the meetings. Meanwhile, the Soviets did little to suppress the growing activity.

Then, without the slightest warning, a bomb tore through a subway station. Tass, the official news agency, announced that the explosion had caused little damage and no injuries. But through various sources we learned that six people had actually been killed and many more badly injured.

There were also reports that a man was seen stuffing a package into a garbage container minutes before the blast. Strangely enough, he left the station escorted by two men and was never arrested.

"It looks like a KGB operation that went haywire," Father said. "I'm sure they planned to blame us, but they didn't intend to kill those people. They must now shape a new strategy. It will be interesting to see what their next move is."

We didn't have to wait long. Two days later, listening to the Voice of America news broadcast, we heard that the subway blast was the work of human-rights activists. "Soviet officials believe the dissidents are taking a different, more violent, approach against their leadership," the announcer said. "In other international developments . . ."

"That story is a plant," Mother said, turning up the volume.

"Of course it is," Father said. "We know the KGB have several foreign reporters in their pocket, but an outsider wouldn't. It's a tactic that will be effective unless we do something. With this tragic bombing, the Soviets can say to the world, 'Look how these so-called human-rights activists act. They bomb innocent commuters. We have no choice but to protect our citizens from these madmen.'"

"But what can you do?" Grandma asked. "Just let the story die, that's my advice."

"No, Mother, we must get the facts out before the world accepts the official explanation," Father said. "I'll go get Georgy and bring him here."

"No!" Mother said. "No meeting in our house. They will be looking for any excuse to break in here. Meet Georgy on the street somewhere. He listens to the news.

He'll know what the problem is. Work out a statement while you walk. I'll go stay with Anna Yakir until you get back." She turned to me. "Put Yulia to bed, please."

Yulia was already asleep on the couch. Her thumb was in her mouth.

"Can't I go with Father?" I asked.

"No, it's too dangerous," Mother said. "Do as you're told."

"Father, please!"

"No, Lev, your mother is right. Stay here."

I'd been out with Father at night before and nothing had happened. Still, I sensed an urgency in my parents' voices that told me now was not the time to make a scene. Besides, if I made a fuss, Yulia would feel obliged to, no matter how sleepy she was.

I went to the couch and picked Yulia up in my arms. Grandma sat in her chair, quiet, a shawl wrapped around her shoulders. Mother and Father were whispering near the door as they put on their coats.

The next morning, reporters came, ready for a story.

Percy was there sitting on the floor with Yulia. He'd brought something for her. It was a doll named Barbie, complete with a wardrobe any Russian would envy.

"We've asked you here for an informal chat," Mother said, turning the radio on loud.

The reporters opened their notebooks.

"We'd prefer this to be off the record, since we don't yet have the information to make a solid accusation. Is that understood? We do not want to see any individual's name associated with what we're about to say until we can verify our intuitions. Is that clear?"

The people in the room nodded, or softly said, "Yes." "Sure." "No problem, off the record."

"You understand our need to be careful," she said.

"You know of the report given about the recent subway blast. It must be obvious to all of you that no dissident would ever plant a bomb. Our aim is to change minds, not take lives. The authorities are hoping to warp world opinion against the democratic movement, hoping for an excuse to repress us even further, looking to destroy our movement, if possible, because they now realize the world is listening to us.

"We've had some success over the last few years. International agreements have opened more opportunities for us. There is pressure on the state to respect our freedom. The world, thanks to your reporting, knows more about human-rights violations in every country—not just our own. That is good. Without international support, we have little hope of ever planting the seeds for a society free from fear and repression. I suspect the KGB and the leadership are afraid of our small successes and will do anything to turn world opinion against us."

A French reporter turned to Father and asked in Russian, "Are you saying that the bomb was planted by the KGB, who hope to blame it on the human-rights movement?"

"We feel it is a good possibility that the bombing was the work of official agents. Yes. Remember: these remarks are off the record. Do not put any individual's name next to this answer, although you can say it came from a human-rights activist."

"If the KGB set off the bomb, why did they wait two days to release the story?" a British journalist asked.

Mother answered, "Our suspicion is they never expected fatalities from the blast. So, in light of the death toll, we imagine they had to reshape their strategy."

"What's your next move?" another reporter asked.

"We must wait and see how this develops," Mother said. "We shall continue to do the work we have always done. Work for the release of people imprisoned solely for their beliefs. Alert the world of violations of international agreements on human rights. Attempt to communicate with the Soviet officials about pending criminal cases we feel the world may not be allowed to know about."

Percy remained after the other foreigners had left. He sat on the couch, pensive, smoking a cigarette.

"May I have one?" Mother asked him.

"Here," he said, reaching into his leather bag. "I brought you a couple more cartons."

Mother took the cartons and put them on the dining table. "Thank you," she said as she unwrapped one of the packs from a carton and took a cigarette. "Have you found Moscow to your liking?"

"To tell you the truth, I'm still having trouble finding my way around. All those squares and intersecting streets are pretty confusing."

"Maybe Lev would show you around," Mother said. "He enjoys practicing his English with Americans." She turned to me. "Lev? Would you like to take Percy on a tour?"

I smiled. "If it means I don't have to set the table, I'd like to."

"Tonight I shall set the table for you," Mother said with a grin. "You two go ahead. Don't be home late, son. We'll eat at our regular time."

Percy and I stopped on the Moskvoretsky Bridge, which crosses the Moska River. It offered a close view of the Kremlin towers and bastions to the north. Above the wall rose the face of the Grand Palace, and behind it the gold and silver spires of the cathedrals looked like treetops.

It was cool on the bridge. The wind didn't bother me.

46

But Percy was shivering in his thin jacket, so we walked up the slope to Red Square.

"Did the Communists build Red Square?" Percy asked.

I smiled, amazed how little most foreigners know about the places they choose to visit. "No. The square is almost as old as the city itself. In the fifteenth century, it was called the *torg*, which means market place. The square has served for executions and for religious ceremonies. It's been the center of Moscow for centuries."

"There's nothing quite like it in America," Percy said, mostly to himself. "I'm cold. Can we get inside?"

"Sure, we can walk through GUM."

So we went toward the east end of Red Square where it is bordered by two large buildings. Before the revolution, they housed shops and offices. Now one is GUM, the state-owned department store, the largest in the U.S.S.R.

Percy told me that in America the store windows are decorated to attract shoppers. That certain stores cater to a certain class of people. That the mannequins look so life-like one waits for them to breathe, and the clothes are colorful—sometimes outrageously so—and sharp-looking—not like those in the U.S.S.R.

Here we have plaster mannequins whose faces need a fresh paint job. The heads are topped by awkward horse-hair wigs. The bodies are supported by a square iron pole between the legs. The limbs fit poorly, leaving joint lines that look like Frankenstein's monster. The faces are lifeless, unfeeling.

In America, Percy told me, the windows are changed every week. Here they change only with the seasons.

In the spring, the overcoats are removed, leaving a plain dark suit. For summer, the jacket is removed, leaving a short-sleeved white shirt. In the fall, a sweater is buttoned on and the jacket is returned. With the first snow comes the overcoat's return for a five-month stay.

47

Walking through the main floor, Percy asked, "Where is all the merchandise?"

"It's on display," I said. "Where do you think it is?"

"This is it?" he asked in horror. "This is the entire selection?"

I had to laugh. Americans delight me at times. They can't believe the rest of the world isn't like home. "Yes, this is it. There are samples to try on for size. Everything else is kept in those stacked boxes behind the counters. You wait in line until one of the women helps you."

In America, Percy told me, no one likes to wait in line for anything. And no shirt comes in less than a dozen different colors. In America, there are rows and rows of colors and patterns filling nearly every inch of floor space. The walls are tiered with rows of goods arranged by size. A person wanting to buy pants, let's say, will have scores of choices in his or her size. There is a wide price range between certain manufacturers.

Here things are much more simple. You just stand in line and wear out of the store what everyone else wears.

How could I explain to Percy Elliman how things are for us? Percy, handsome and healthy, dressed in expensive clothes.

We came to the area of GUM that sold plaster statues of Marx and Lenin. Here there was some selection, the sizes ranging from small enough to attach to the dashboard of an automobile to large enough to be put on top of a building and seen for blocks.

"What are these for?" Percy asked.

"I'm not sure, to tell you the truth," I said.

Percy walked over to a bust of Lenin that was four times life-size. It came up to Percy's chest. "Is this solid?"

"How should I know?"

Before I could stop him, Percy planted several knocks

48

squarely in the middle of Lenin's bald white scalp. The sound reverberated. Store workers looked on in horror.

Percy looked at me, laughing at the results of his curiosity. I grabbed his arm and started to lead him to the nearest exit.

"You shouldn't have done that, Percy," I told him.

"Why not?" he asked, studying the people's surprised expressions as we rushed by.

"Because we can get in trouble, that's why!"

"For *that*? Come on, it was funny."

I stopped and looked at him. "Funny? You think the authorities have a sense of humor?"

Percy stared at me, his grin gone. "I guess knowing about the situation here and experiencing it first hand is still new to me. I'm sorry Lev."

When we returned to the street, people were leaving the office buildings, another work day at its end. Everyone was in a hurry, rushing to the bus stop to stand in line, waiting for an already crowded bus to pull up.

"I have something at my hotel for you, if you have time," Percy said. "I don't want you to be late for supper. Maybe we can take a taxi?"

"We'll never get one at this time. I'm not in that big of a rush, but it'll be faster if we walk," I told him.

So we walked along the crowded streets. People jostled us as we passed them. The sun was low in the sky, dropping the temperature. I could see Percy had not adjusted to our weather. His face was red, his nose running, his arms held tight to his sides.

We arrived at the Metropole Hotel, one of Moscow's finest and used primarily by Westerners. We took the elevator to Percy's floor, where he picked up his key from the clerk stationed near the stairs.

Percy's hotel room was the most luxurious place I had

ever visited. It was so bright: chandeliers everywhere, one on either side of the double-size bed and another directly above it—maybe tourists are too tired to reach over to the side when they finally put down their travel guides and go to sleep. The walls were pastel blue. Reproductions of paintings from the Hermitage—Russia's foremost museum —were evenly spaced above a walnut dresser large enough for my family to store all our clothes in.

"Make yourself comfortable," Percy said. "I'm going to take a quick shower."

"Can I use the toilet first?" I asked, wanting to see the bathroom.

"Sure, help yourself."

The bathroom was as large as our living room. I looked at myself in the large mirror from every conceivable angle, flushed the toilet so Percy would not be suspicious, and returned to the other room.

Percy was naked, scratching himself. He walked past me, patting me on the back on his way to the shower.

I didn't dare touch anything, so I sat on the bed until he reemerged. His hair was dripping wet. A towel was draped around his shoulders.

"Nothing like a hot shower to renew me after a long day." He went to the dresser to get a pair of underwear, which he slipped into, then he pulled a robe from the bottom drawer.

I don't know why I was so embarrassed. I had seen naked people before, but I couldn't understand why Percy was acting so familiar around me. I felt "young" for my age; most of the other boys were already shaving. I had little use for a razor. "I think I'd better be heading home," I said.

Percy stared at me for a moment, then said, "Your father is in a real tough spot, isn't he? I think I know how

50

you feel. One of these days they're going to arrest him. Then what are you going to do?"

What could I say? "Wait and see what happens" was the best I could respond.

I lowered my head, not wanting to return Percy's stare. Finally he squeezed my shoulder, as if that would make my troubles disappear, and said, "I've got something for you, remember?" He went to the closet to pull out a suitcase from which he removed a large manila envelope. "Here."

I sat on the bed and opened the envelope, taking out a thick magazine with a beautiful woman on the slick cover. Inside were dozens of other women wearing little or no clothing. They were photographed in all sorts of strange positions. Some were sitting in chairs smiling, their eyes closed, tongues out. Others were wearing slinky nightgowns and didn't look sleepy. And they couldn't keep their legs together. They had their hands on themselves. Shoulders back, chests out. Friendly and not ashamed. I had never seen anything like it.

With my hands shaking slightly, I put the magazine back in the envelope and left it on the bed.

"Take it," Percy said, "it's yours." Then he winked at me. "Just don't let your parents find it."

"I can't take this."

"Sure you can. Every warm-blooded boy in America has a stack of them under his bed for easy reference."

"Things are different here, Percy," I said.

"You mean you've never had a woman, is that it?"

"I have a girl friend, Tanya Yakir, but we're in no hurry."

"Why not? Listen, you're old enough. You're what . . . fourteen, fifteen?"

"Sixteen," I said.

"Well, if I were you, I'd let Tanya know you're ready. She's probably just waiting for you to make the move, believe me."

"I've tried," I said, "but she makes me stop."

Percy came over and sat down next to me. "You've kissed her, haven't you?"

"Sometimes, yes, in the hallway of my building. It's the only place we can have some privacy."

"And what else?"

"What else what?"

"What else have you done?" Percy asked. "Gotten up her shirt yet?"

"Yes, for a little while." I couldn't believe he was asking me such questions. He was so different with me than when he was at my home. Maybe he was trying to be friendly. I knew Americans had a reputation for openness; still, I felt uncomfortable talking to him about Tanya. "Tanya is a very nice girl."

Percy nodded. "They're all nice girls. Well, I hope Tanya comes around."

I sat there, staring at the floor, not knowing what to say.

Percy got up to get a cigarette. He stood against the wall, smoking, looking at me. "I hope everything is okay," he finally said. "I was just trying to be nice. I thought maybe you needed someone to talk to about things you couldn't talk to your parents about. I'm sorry, Lev, if I upset you. I realize now I shouldn't have expected an easy time between us. It's just I see you at your parents' home— and I guess I see myself in you. In a world not of your own creation, in the middle of a crisis that will affect you even though it mainly concerns your parents." He took a long drag on his cigarette. "I'm really sorry. Let's leave it that I've been in your place. When my father was . . . well, when he couldn't work anymore, I, too, suddenly found myself an outsider at school. A lot of my old friends would no longer have anything to do with me. Not that I had done anything, only because I belonged to a certain family. Anyway, know I'm here for you if and when you need to talk."

"What happened to your father?" I asked.

"My father? He was blacklisted in the early 1950s. By that I mean he was labeled a Communist sympathizer at a time when emotions against the Soviet Union were very high in America. Many politicians in America took advantage of the so-called cold war and conducted hearings into supposed Communist infiltration of various American industries, especially show business. Dad . . . my father was a film director. Everyone liked his work. But he never worked again and . . . he started to drink. It was a long time ago, so I guess I have some perspective on it now. He left us, deserted us—a victim of his own paranoia as much as of the colleagues who turned him in." Percy sighed. "These things happen in America, too, I'm sorry to say."

"I'd better be going," I said, standing up. I headed for the door.

"Here, take this," Percy said, picking up the magazine, "if you want it."

I left the hotel, the magazine flat against my belly under my shirt and belt. I took the bus home and tried to sneak into my room without being noticed. But Father and Grandma were sitting at the table when I arrived.

"Mama tells us you're a tour guide now, son," Father kidded.

"Yes, I guess so." I knew that I might get caught and my heart was beating loudly, the magazine sticking to my stomach. I was afraid to move for fear it would squeak and expose me. "I'd better wash up."

"So how's Percy?" Grandma asked. "A nice man?"

What a time to want a conversation. "He's fine, I guess." I was trying to hold my stomach in, afraid the magazine was creating a rectangular bulge under my shirt.

"Okay, son, better clean up for supper," Father said.

I went to our room and closed the door so Yulia wouldn't walk in on me. I pulled the magazine free and was about to hide it under my mattress when I decided to take one last quick look before going to the bathroom. I glanced over the pictures, trying to impose Tanya's willing face on the glossy, fleshy bodies.

8

One of the "journalists" who attended the press conference about the bombing must have been a KGB agent, for Father was phoned the next day and ordered to appear at the Municipal Procuracy. Our phone rarely operates. But when the authorities call, they have no problem getting through to us.

My parents started to talk. I was certain they'd once again tell me as little as possible, so I went into my room to leave them alone.

I sat on the floor next to Yulia, who was dressing her new doll to look like a tiny airline stewardess.

"Doesn't she look nice?" Yulia asked.

"Yes, very nice," I said, trying to ignore Yulia. I was wondering if my parents would come get me. After all, I was sixteen years old. My parents were deciding my fate, as well as their own. Might not something I had to say matter?

"You're not even looking, Lev," Yulia said, hurt. "You can't see anything unless you look."

There was a knock at the door. No doubt it was Father saying goodbye.

"Come in," I said.

The door swung open. Father was putting on his coat. Mother stood behind him.

"I know it's Sunday and you have schoolwork to do," he said, "but Mama and I have been talking. We think you should come with me to the Procuracy. I know you feel we've ignored the fact that you're a young man with a good, quick mind. Perhaps you're right. Understand, this is not a simple mission. The procurator will no doubt give us a stiff warning. He'll try to scare us with all types of threats. Mama and I think you can handle it. Do you want to come?"

I had my coat on in no time. I was glad to go, not really thinking about what the procurator might say. What was important was that my parents had acknowledged I counted, that I was an adult, no longer a child in their eyes. Even then, however, I knew there was a trade-off. I was once and for all turning in the safety of childlike ignorance for a place in a world where games were played for keeps. For the first time I was meeting face to face with a powerful Soviet official.

After an hour's wait, we were escorted to the offices of the Deputy Procurator General of the U.S.S.R., I. V. Akakievich. In his office were two other men.

"Good morning, Comrade Kolokol, I am Akakievich, Chief of the Procuracy's Investigation Section." He remained seated but extended his hand across the desk for Father to shake.

Every gesture was to be a test of will, and Father made

no effort to reach for his hand. Akakievich quickly moved his hand toward a pack of cigarettes, as if that was what he was after in the first place.

"I might suggest your son waits in the outer office," Akakievich said.

"You have your men here. I want mine," Father said.

I didn't smile, but hearing this made me happy.

"As you wish, Comrade. I have a boy about your son's age," Akakievich said, turning a framed photograph of his family so we could see it.

"So we have established we are both family men," Father said.

"My boy is planning a military career," Akakievich said, studying the photograph. "How about yours?"

"Lev Kolokol can speak for himself," Father said.

Akakievich asked me, "So, Lev, you are a bright boy, from all reports. How do you plan to serve the state?"

"I hope to live in a society that will allow me a choice of service," I said. I was nervous but tried to speak up clearly.

Akakievich smiled and shook his finger accusingly at us. "He is very much the son of Sergei Ivanovich."

"I don't imagine you asked us here for a social chat. What is the purpose of disrupting our lives?" Father asked.

"Then I shall speak with no further amenities, Comrade Kolokol." Akakievich opened a file folder thick with papers. "The purpose of the summons is to give you an official warning. We have long been acquainted with—and distressed by—your and your wife's activities."

I looked at Father, who failed to change his expression.

Akakievich continued, scanning a report, "Yesterday you addressed a meeting of foreigners in your home. You issued a statement that will be used as hostile anti-Soviet propaganda by our enemies. In your statement, read by your wife acting as your mouthpiece, you mentioned that

57

the recent explosion in our subway system was the work of state agencies."

He look up from the file, attempting to reprimand Father with a stare. Like a strict teacher letting an unruly pupil know the depth of his misconduct, he spoke slowly and sternly. "Comrade Kolokol, you further alleged that the blast was falsely linked to associates of yours in the hope of changing public opinion. Do you deny that you issued such a statement?"

"What is it that you want, Deputy Procurator?" Father asked.

"You are required to disavow your scandalous lies. Please sign a correction my office has prepared which will be published in *Izvestia* for all to read."

Father shook his head from side to side.

"I remind you, Sergei Kolokol, this is not your first hostile and criminally anti-Soviet action. We have remained tolerant since we hoped you might still make a contribution to the people's struggle. But you've continued to abuse our patience. Today I am presenting you with a formal and very serious warning. Look it over and sign. This is both my personal advice and a legal request."

He stood up and handed Father a piece of paper.

Leaning toward me so I could see, Father read the document out loud:

" 'Citizen S. I. Kolokol is hereby warned that he has issued a deliberately false statement in which he alleged that the explosion in the Moscow subway station was an official action devised by government agencies directed against so-called dissidents. Citizen S. I. Kolokol is warned, and understands, that the continuation of his criminal acts will result in his liability in accordance with the law of the land.' "

Akakievich had put his signature on the bottom of the document. There remained a blank line for Father's.

Father put the paper back on the desk, then leaned

back and put his hands in his lap. "I refuse to sign. I never said the KGB was responsible for the bomb. What I expressed was my concern that the government would use the explosion as an excuse to illegally crack down on innocent people trying to live their lives under internationally accepted precepts of human rights."

"Citizen Kolokol, am I to assume this is your response?" Akakievich said, his lower lip protruding. I don't believe he really thought Father would sign.

Father stood, put his hand on the desk, and leaned toward Akakievich. "I remind you that the KGB has never publicly acknowledged responsibility for countless crimes against the citizens it is supposed to protect. The world is just starting to learn the extent of your criminality." Father straightened up, crossing his arms in front of his chest. "I want a copy of this document for my records. It is not marked classified, so I am entitled to a copy under law."

Akakievich took a deep breath, opened his drawer, and removed a pen, which he extended toward Father. "Sign, please."

"I refuse."

"Sign for your family, Comrade."

"Leave my family out of this," Father said sharply. "They are of no concern here. This 'warning' is your affair."

"No, Comrade, it is *your* affair." Akakievich stood up, meeting Father eye to eye. "Treat this warning with utmost seriousness. You know the dissemination of false, anti-Soviet statements is punishable by law. We do not arrest someone for nothing."

"My experience shows otherwise," Father said.

Again Akakievich turned to me. "Lev, tell me, why does your father act so unreasonably?"

"Do not think you can use my son against me," Father said, putting his arm out as if to stop me from speaking.

I had no intention of speaking. What could I say?

"It is impossible for me to sign a document that labels my actions as criminal," Father continued. "And I will continue my activities in accordance with my conscience."

"For how much longer, Citizen Kolokol?" Akakievich questioned.

"May we go?" Father asked.

Akakievich waved us off without speaking.

The meeting had lasted only a few minutes.

"Sergei, you've made *Izvestia*," Grandma said. "They're hoping to discredit you."

"It is to be expected," Father said, looking up from his writing.

Mother was seated on the couch. Yulia was curled up, her head resting in Mother's lap.

"Lev honey, you read it. I don't have my glasses." Grandma handed me *Izvestia*, the official government newspaper.

"The headline is 'A SLANDERER IS WARNED,'" I began. "'S. I. Kolokol was summoned to the Procuracy of the U.S.S.R. I. V. Akakievich, Deputy Procurator General of the U.S.S.R. and State Counselor of Justice, First Class, warned Kolokol he was responsible for deliberately false slanderous inventions which discredit the Soviet state and social system. If Kolokol ignores the warning issued him, he will be held criminally responsible before Soviet law.'"

I folded the newspaper and gently placed it on top of the pile my parents kept for clippings.

Father raised an eyebrow. "Why just a warning, Irina?" he asked Mother. "What's their thinking?"

"Perhaps the Kremlin is involved in some trade talks with the West which might be upset if they arrested you," she said. "No way of knowing for certain."

Grandma looked at her old hands, shaking her head

slightly. "Sergei Ivanovich, it's only a question of time before they come for you."

"Everything is only a question of time, Mama," he said.

Mother gently shook Yulia until she awoke. Yulia sat up, rubbing her eyes.

"Time for dinner," Mother said, getting up. "We all need our strength."

9

Father began to stay up late into the night, gave less time to Yulia and me, even forsook his afternoon walks—all in an effort to accelerate work on his manuscript. We had no way of knowing when or how the Soviets would further isolate him from the dissident community, if his arrest was imminent, or if they were merely starting a campaign to harass and discredit him. But we knew the kinds of actions taken against him—the summoning to the Procuracy, the slanderous attack in the newspaper—had preceded the arrest of other activists; there was no reason to think Father's fate would be different.

Several days after the *Izvestia* article appeared, Georgy

came over to remind Father we had promised to attend Passover dinner at Mochol Pevrod's that night.

"Irina and the children will come. Georgy, you are my dear friend, but I myself haven't the time to give up an evening," Father said. "My duty is to my work at this point."

"Duty? Don't talk to me of duty!" Georgy shouted. I couldn't remember seeing him so angry, especially at Father. "We have a higher duty than to our time and cause. We have a duty to God. If our friendship, our children, our faith in liberty means anything to you, Sergei Ivanovich, you will be there this evening."

Father stared at Georgy, then rose and embraced him. "Yes, you are right. I will come."

Georgy patted Father on the back, then looked at me. "Your duty, Lev," he said with a smile, "is to translate for your friend Mr. Elliman, whom I want you to invite. Make him feel at home."

I had never seen Mochol Pevrod's tiny apartment so clean. Usually there were papers and books scattered around the room, dust everywhere. When one sat down on her sofa, a cloud would whirl into the air. But not tonight. As part of the preparations for Passover, Mochol had cleaned the apartment from ceiling to floor and set a wonderful table, using her special dishes.

As the streets became dark outside the living room windows, Georgy began to recite from memory, " 'And ye shall observe the feast of unleavened bread; for in this selfsame day have I brought your hosts out of the land of Egypt; therefore shall ye observe this day throughout your generations by an ordinance forever.' " He stretched out his arms toward us. "Shalom. Welcome. On behalf of our hostess, Mochol Pevrod, I welcome you to our Passover seder. I hope everyone can hear me over the radio, for the story of our deliverance is a wonderful occasion to come together. As was commanded in the Book of Exodus, every year Jews gather to retell the story of their liberation from slavery. It's wonderful to see our dear friends the Kolokols here, and we welcome a newcomer, Mr. Percy Elliman, to our seder and hope he will be patient with us."

"I'm happy to be here," Percy said, after I explained to him what Georgy had said.

Georgy then continued: "Now, Mochol, please begin our seder with the lighting of the candles."

Mochol stood up, adjusted her shawl, and lit two long candles that were placed in front of her. She recited some words in Hebrew, joined by Anna and Tanya, then said for the rest of us to hear: "By lighting festive lights we praise God, by whom all life is sacred. We kindle a light of sanctity, a light of freedom and hope, which no oppressor has ever or will ever extinguish."

Since my family was not religious, the service was both mysterious and inspiring. Not being Jewish, I really couldn't understand all that occurred during the night, couldn't fully appreciate how it brought home to the present the long struggle of a people for their emancipation. Still, any ceremony about a people's liberation from oppression struck an emotional chord in me, especially because religious freedom is not tolerated here. Freedom has many consequences, among them thanksgiving, revelry, and a serious consideration of what it really means to be released from either physical or psychological bondage. To take part in the celebration of this struggle, in the retelling of the story of a people who would not knuckle under to tyranny made it a special evening.

Tanya and her family took the occasion with a mixture of devotion and celebration, mirroring the mood of the service. When I looked across the table I was glad Percy was there. Although he couldn't understand much of what was said, I was certain the evening would tell him more about our struggle than any sightseeing or long talk ever could.

The empty chair must have had special significance for Mochol, for her husband, Lazar Pevrod, was currently serving a sentence in Vladimir Prison. His crime? He tried to organize an exhibition of contemporary artists whose works were considered nonconformist by the Soviets and, therefore, not exhibited. Lazar Pevrod was sentenced to twelve years for attempting to bring nonofficial art to the public.

"Now we are ready for *Kos Kiddush*, the First Cup of Wine," Georgy said, raising his glass. "During the service we drink four glasses of wine. I know this is the part of the seder that Lev, for one, likes the best." Georgy recited a prayer in Hebrew, then translated it for us. " 'We praise you, O God of the Universe, who creates the fruit of the vine, who has kept us in life, sustained us, and brought us to this festive season.' Now, all drink up."

The wineglasses were quite large, placed on a saucer, and filled to the top. I picked up my glass and swallowed every last drop before putting it down.

"I can see why you like that part," Percy said to me, wiping his mouth.

"It's time for *Karpas*, the parsley, which reminds us of the glories of growth and renewal. Tanya, please recite from the Song of Songs."

Tanya smiled, closed her eyes, and spoke in a soft voice. " 'Rise up, my love, my fair one, and come away. For, lo, the winter is past, the rain is over and gone; The flowers appear on the earth; the time of the singing of birds is come, and the voice of the turtle is heard in our land.' " She opened her eyes and looked at me. " 'Arise, my love, my fair one, and come away. My beloved is mine, and I am his: he feedeth among the lilies.' "

"Lev, you're blushing!" Yulia said, as if I weren't already embarrassed.

Georgy laughed. "This is to be expected at springtime!"

I looked around the table. Everyone was smiling, except Mother, who was shaking her head.

"Come on, Irina, you were young once," Mochol scolded her.

"Remember our trip to the Crimea, when we were first married?" Father asked Mother.

"Sergei Ivanovich, I don't think this is the time . . ."

"I, too, am thinking of springtime," he said, getting up. He went behind Mother, took her head in his hand, reached over, and kissed her.

"Yes, we all remember springtime," Georgy said, raising his eyebrows. "But if we don't proceed, we'll be here until *next* springtime!"

"Georgy, my dear friend, I couldn't help myself," Father said, returning to his seat.

Georgy recited a prayer, then we dipped the parsley in salt water before eating it.

"At seder, when I first taste the parsley and salt water, it brings back every seder I've ever attended," Anna said. "The happy ones spent with my grandparents—my grandfather taking all night, reciting every last word of the service. The terrible ones when Georgy was away. Last year's, just after Natasha was born." Although she was smiling, Anna wiped a tear from her eye. "I love our seders, Mochol. I love the company, the good food, the hope. Tonight, like every Passover, brings all the years together. I look around and see not only those here, but all those now gone. I feel warm and full of love."

Tanya leaned over and kissed her mother.

We then heard the retelling of the story of the Exodus from Egypt, how the Egyptians suffered terrible plagues because of their initial refusal to free the Jews. How Moses led his people away from slavery toward the promised land.

Tanya recited the traditional Four Questions, asking what made Passover such a special observance. Georgy told her the reasons, establishing again the link between the generations stretching back thousands of years.

It was getting late, and I was getting hungry. Still, the time went by swiftly, what with stories and songs and prayers.

" 'We shall remember it was we who were slaves,' " Georgy recited, " 'we who were strangers.' Therefore, we recall these words from Exodus, 'And a stranger shalt thou not oppress; for ye know the heart of a stranger, seeing ye were strangers in the land of Egypt.' " The glasses were filled for the second time. A prayer was recited, and we drank.

"*Shulhan oreih*, the meal is served," Mochol said, getting up to go to the kitchen.

Soon the table was full of food. Everything was delicious: chicken and onions and carrots. All of us ate heartily, as if it was our first meal that day.

"This may sound corny," Percy said, while we waited for dessert, "but tonight, in fact my whole time in Moscow, makes me realize how lucky we are in America. I mean, how free we are to think and act without the fear of always being watched."

"You know how dependent we are on the West for what little freedom we have," Mother said. "Without your interest, there is no telling what the authorities might do. As bad as things are now, if you can imagine, they were much worse when Sergei Ivanovich and I were growing up. So much of the repression we still suffer is the result of those dark days of Stalin's rule. Then to be different from anyone else was to stand out. To stand out was to call attention to yourself. And if you did this, you could depend on one day being arrested and sent away forever. It was a terrible time, when your best friend might turn you in as easily as your worst enemy would. Yes, Percy, you are lucky to have your heritage of liberty in the West."

"I agree with what you said, but we still have a lot of problems in America."

Mother smiled. "If only we had your problems."

"But our problems are real, nonetheless," Percy said.

"No question. But America is still a young nation and it has the problems of an adolescent. It wants desperately to be popular. It wants to prove how big and strong and masculine it is. Like a teenager, it has a short, selective memory and a sense of its own rightness. Russia is old and set in its ways. We have a history of survival. America has not yet proved that it does, I'm afraid."

"Well, even in my lifetime I've seen events that prove America will not only survive, but will continue to grow. Of course, there have been exceptions . . ." Percy picked up his fork and slowly stirred it on his empty plate. "My father was denounced as a Red in the early 1950s. He had joined some political group when he was in college in the 1930s; many people had. How could he know that that association would come back and haunt him? They took away his work and, I think, also took away his life . . . But look at the Vietnam War, at Watergate. Both were terrible episodes in our history and we survived. It's still not clear if America is stronger morally because of these tragedies, but we're still free."

As interesting as it was to listen to Percy speak about America, I had hoped to avoid politics for one evening at least. All the talk did little more than reinforce our sense of integrity and rightness; it wouldn't change our lives. And tonight I wanted to drink wine and be with Tanya.

"Would it be all right if I excused myself for a short walk? I'm really full."

68

"We have to finish the service, Lev," Georgy said, "but go ahead. Just don't be too long."

I stood up and looked across the table at Tanya. "Want to come along?"

"Father?"

"Yes, go ahead. But be careful."

It was cold out. Tanya and I walked briskly to a small park near Mochol's apartment. We sat down on a bench under a bright streetlight. I put my arms around her and brought her toward me.

"What are you doing?" she asked.

"Doing?"

"You may think it's springtime, but I don't! I'm freezing. This is neither the time nor the place . . ."

"Come on, everyone does it in the park."

"Does what?"

"Don't play games, Tanya. I just want to kiss you."

She pulled away from me. "Lev, you have a one-track mind! It's too cold out."

Now both of us were upset. What fantasies I had had of going to the park and doing what I've seen other couples do there were fading from my mind. Why were things so difficult? I stared ahead, shaking my head.

Tanya wrapped her hand around my arm and leaned against me. "Please understand. I don't want to get close and then have to lose each other. I'd rather wait and come together when we have our lives squarely before us. Now we don't. We don't know if my family will be broken up, or yours, or worse. Can you understand? Maybe one day we will have time, but not now, Lev."

I looked down the walk. The next streetlight was clouded with a cold fog. Running through various things to say in my mind, I couldn't decide on one, so remained silent. I was angry, frustrated.

"We'd better get back," she said, standing up. She

reached to take my hand and we walked back to Mochol's in silence.

When we returned to the table, I could see the tone of the evening had changed. Everyone was solemn. At first I thought maybe I had done something, that Tanya and I had been the sole topic of conversation since we left.

"What's wrong?" Tanya said, asking the question I, too, wanted the answer for.

"Percy talked to Simon Reese last night," Mother said. "It is as we feared. Simon said the embassy received information that the authorities are going to intensify their campaign against us. The subway bombing, the warning to Sergei Ivanovich, were only their first assaults."

"Mother told Percy about my history of human-rights violations," Father added. "He's agreed to help Simon get it out of the country. But it's in no shape to be published at this time. We have to finish it as quickly as possible."

"But first we have a higher duty to perform; we have a seder to complete," Georgy said, standing up. "The Third Glass of Wine."

The rest of the service stretched on. The bad news Percy had brought seemed to alter time itself. The prayers seemed longer, more obtuse. The songs were sung with less heart than before.

Then came time for *Kos Eliyahu*, the Cup of Elijah.

"How many images the memory of the Prophet Elijah stirs in us," Georgy said. "The times when we were objects of ridicule, when our homes were under constant surveillance, when hateful and stupid men forced our doors with terror." He turned to Tanya. "Please open the door so Elijah can enter."

Tanya stood up and opened the door.

"As is written in the Book of Malachi, 'Behold, I will send you Elijah the prophet before the coming of the great and dreadful day of the Lord: And he shall turn the heart of the fathers to the children, and the heart of the children to their fathers.' "

Everyone watched the cup of wine in the center of the table. The cool air from the hallway breezed in, gently rippling the wine.

"You can close the door now," Georgy told Tanya.

She sat down. Soon the room returned to normal. I looked at the glass and could swear the level of the wine in Elijah's cup had lowered.

Everyone was smiling. That moment returned a magic to the night. By the end of the service—and one more glass of wine—a feeling of celebration or thanksgiving had been restored.

It was well past midnight when Georgy closed the seder. "For all people, this, our hope: next year in Jerusalem! Next year, may all be free!"

"This was a marvelous experience," Percy said. "Thank you for including me."

"We have one last thing to do, a tradition in the Yakir family. Come!" Georgy pushed his chair back and motioned us away from the table, to the only area in the apartment where there was room to move around. "A dance to praise the Almighty! A dance for freedom and love!"

We formed a circle, our arms around one another's shoulders. I stood between Father and Percy. Tanya and Mother faced me. Yulia and even Natasha, held in Anna's arms, joined the circle.

We started to move to the right, at first slowly, gradually faster. The Yakirs were singing in Hebrew, a joyous, upbeat song. We stamped our feet down on the beat, going around and round. Faster and faster we went, holding one another close. The room spinning behind us, our heads light from wine and the revolutions.

For one wonderful moment I was certain we would leave the ground and whirl in our circle to the sky.

10

As if an impossible assignment were due in too short a time to complete, everyone was so busy there was hardly time to eat or sleep. Our apartment had been transformed into an intellectual sweatshop as my parents did little but write and type for hours on end. Father worked all day, and arriving home from work, Mother only went to the toilet before sitting down at the table. Friends dropped by when they could. Everyone shared the sense of time running out.

I offered to help, but my parents would not hear of it. Father leaned back in his chair. "Lev, please, I'm trying to concentrate. You know I have to finish my history as soon as possible."

"But I want to help," I said. "I thought we were in this as a family."

"Lev, son, don't argue, please," Father said, "not now. There is too much work to do. Please go along with your mother and me on this. We know where everything is. No matter how good your intentions, I'm afraid you'd only be in the way."

"If you want to help, go into the kitchen and ask Grandma what she needs from the store," Mother said. "That would be the biggest help right now. And why don't you take Yulia along for a walk. By the way, Malsa is coming over to help later tonight. I know she'll be happy to see you."

I did as I was told. I took Yulia to the store, where we bought bread and cheese. I held her hand, quickly walking down the street, aware of the distance between us and the agents following us.

"Lev, tell those men to go away," Yulia said, craning her neck to watch the agents. "Who are they?"

"Shhh! Don't look at them!" I yanked her forward, mad at her, but at the same time recognizing myself asking the same questions when I was her age.

Back home, I sliced the bread and cheese and put water on to boil.

"I'll take care of the tea," Grandma said. "Take the food into the other room."

I put the plate down between Mother and Father. Then I picked up the introduction Father had been proofreading. " 'Dissent is not a form of violent revolution. Dissent is a matter of communication. Only when opposing views are known to other people do they become important and politically significant. This is especially the case under our Soviet system, which defines *any* criticism as a crime against the state.

" 'We do not ask for revolution. We ask only for

glasnost', the free and open distribution of ideas and information. Only when thinking people have new information can we expect to increase their political consciousness.

" 'The history of dissent in Russia is a long and honored one, even through centuries of autocratic rule. Like our predecessors, we must be both watchdog and critic of the present regime. The government must look to our educated peers to fill its many bureaucratic positions. It is this group we must hope will at least consider the facts.' "

Yulia was in the kitchen with Grandma. They were baking cookies for Yulia's birthday party the following day.

Was I the only one who thought it was crazy to be planning a child's birthday party in the midst of all the threats and tensions?

I felt like leaving, going over to see Tanya. I wasn't serving any purpose at home. But I sensed I should be around, so I went to the couch and tried to read my school assignment.

When Malsa arrived, there was no time for polite talk; she sat down next to Father, proofreading for the last time the pages he had finished.

The radio was on loud. Father's temper was short. He rarely kept his feelings inside among family and close friends. "What are you doing?" he shouted at Malsa when she wrote something on one of his pages.

"Sergei Ivanovich, I'm only trying to make this sentence clearer."

"Your job is to proofread, understand? Not rewrite!"

His shouting brought Grandma out of the kitchen.

"Your voice is too loud," she told Father. "The neighbors will hear you."

Father touched Malsa's arm. "I'm sorry. I know you are doing your best."

The tension was eased with Georgy's visit. He kissed everyone—as usual—yet he looked distraught, upset like the others.

Georgy left his wet coat downstairs and accepted a towel from Grandma. "Dry your hair, Georgy dear," she told him, "or you'll catch your death."

"My splendid Grandma, what would I do without you? Between you and my wife, I can't get away with anything," Georgy said with a grin. He walked around, stopping to touch Father on the shoulder. "So, Sergei Ivanovich, how is the work coming?"

"Behind schedule, as always."

"How are you, Georgy?" Mother asked.

"Besides the four KGB thugs watching my home, besides my telephone which no longer works, besides my mail which arrives already open, besides my daughter who has a cold thanks to the rain, I can't complain." Georgy picked up a piece of paper. He nodded his head as he returned the page to its pile. Then he kiddingly pinched Father's cheek. "Sergei Ivanovich, you are a saint. And if you're not a saint now, you will be after I arrive in heaven and talk to those in charge."

Georgy opened his shirt to remove a folder, which he placed on the table. "Here are my updated sections, ready for typing."

"Can I get you a cup of tea?" Grandma asked him.

"No, I want to be home with my family," he said. "I will see you tomorrow for Yulia's celebration."

"I don't know if we'll have time for her party," Mother said. "As it is, we'll be busy all night."

"Irina, find the time for Yulia," he said, putting his hand on her shoulder. "It's important—not only for the child, but for us. We must not let the authorities know they've gotten to us. Besides, I'm ready for a party. See you tomorrow."

75

"Goodbye, my friend," Father said, "and be careful on your way home."

"I'm always careful," Georgy said with a wink.

When I got home from school the next day, I helped Mother set the table for the party. By the time we had put out the sweets, people started arriving.

Percy came with a big box for Yulia.

"Can I open it now?" she asked.

"Don't you want to wait for your other presents?" Mother asked.

"No," Yulia said, tearing off the wrapping. Inside was a stuffed bear. "I'll name him Percy the bear."

"Thanks, I always wanted to have a bear named after me," Percy said with a grin.

We waited over an hour for the Yakirs to arrive. Finally we went ahead and ate the sweets and sang songs. Everyone was worried about the Yakirs, but we made the best of the afternoon for Yulia's sake.

By seven o'clock we still hadn't heard from them. All of the guests had left, even Percy.

Father tried to call their apartment, but the phone was out.

At nine o'clock, Anna finally arrived.

"Georgy never came home from the museum," she told us.

"Where's Tanya?" I asked.

"She's home with Natasha."

"Have you called the museum?" Father asked.

"Our phone doesn't work," Anna said. "I went there and they claimed he hadn't been there all day. A lie, of course."

"There's nothing we can do," Mother said. "Come on, Anna, we'll walk you home. You should be with your girls."

"I hope I didn't ruin your party," Anna said, stooping

down to Yulia. "Happy birthday, darling," Anna said, hugging her.

My parents were gone for hours. I felt trapped. I knew I should stay home, but I wanted to go look for them. I stood by the window, but all I saw were the agents across the street. The apartment was so quiet. And I felt helpless.

"Put your sister to bed," Grandma told me. "I'm going to bed, too. There's nothing we can do."

"There must be something!"

"Lev, I have lived a great many years." She shook her head. "There's nothing."

I was in bed, unable to sleep, when my parents returned. They went to bed without much noise, but I could hear them talking quietly.

Then I saw the hall light go on and saw shadows under my door.

Both Mother and Father entered our room. Mother went to Yulia's bed to rearrange the blanket, which had slid to the floor. She pulled it up and tucked it in, then leaned over to stroke Yulia's forehead, clearing the hair from her eyes. Yulia woke up briefly, just to touch Mother's arm for a moment before falling asleep again.

Father sat on my bed.

"Did Georgy come home?" I asked.

"I'm afraid . . . I'm afraid not." Father said.

"How's Tanya?" I asked.

"Worried, of course."

"Did she ask for me?" I wondered.

"No, Lev, she had more important things on her mind."

"What do you think happened?"

"I don't know," he said. He stared at me, his shoulders slumped forward, his breathing shallow. Then he turned to Mother and quietly asked, "Irina, what are those lines by Yeats?"

She seemed to know exactly which ones he couldn't remember. " 'Things fall apart; the center cannot hold; /

Mere anarchy is loosed upon the world, / The blood-dimmed tide is loosed, and everywhere / The ceremony of innocence is drowned; / The best lack all conviction, while the worst / Are full of passionate intensity.' " She was standing as if lost in a blizzard, her arms crisscrossed over her chest, her body shaking slightly.

Suddenly Father leaned forward to lift me into an embrace. I remember thinking how strong he was to pull me from my bed. I remember the power of his hug. And I remember feeling his face wet with tears.

11

The news was delivered in the morning by a phone caller who refused to identify himself. "Georgy Yakir has been killed in an accident" was all he told Father.

"Accident?" Father said. "What kind of accident?"

"A fatal one," the caller said before quickly disconnecting.

Mother stood in the kitchen doorway, frozen. I was sitting at the table, now afraid to move. When Father put the receiver back in its cradle, he lifted his hand to his eyes, and told us what the caller had said.

Grandma was the first to speak. "Sergei Ivanovich, we must do something. They are shooting you down one by one as the world does nothing."

"We'll use our home for a memorial service," Father said quietly, trying to compose himself. "We must not let Georgy be forgotten as so many have. We will include the Western press, but it is him we shall honor—not our cause."

I thought about Tanya, who was so close to her father. I wanted to hold her, to feel something alive and loving against me. It was as if Georgy's death created a rift between my parents' generation and mine. Of course I loved them, but they had had their lives. Gone to the university and married. Had careers and children. Lived together until their every gesture was known to each other. My own life had barely unfolded. I needed to see Tanya.

I knew Georgy. I had touched him. Now so had death. Would Father be next? Waiting, with nowhere to escape, until someone pushed a button and ordered him gone?

Mother took a step forward but then stopped and raised fists to either side of her head, as if she had to lash out at something. Then, staring at Father, she spoke with an uncommon edge in her voice. "And who will speak at your memorial service, Sergei Ivanovich Kolokol?"

Fifteen people squeezed into our apartment.

Most of the faces were familiar: friends of my parents and the Yakirs, Mochol Pevrod, Western reporters, including Percy. One face belonged to a stranger who I suspect was a KGB agent.

There was room for only a few chairs. These went to Grandma, Mochol, Anna Yakir, and Natasha, who smiled throughout the service, excited by the attention she was receiving from so many strangers. Tanya stood next to her, occasionally reaching down to try to keep Natasha in her seat.

Without saying a word, I went over to stand next to Tanya. She looked at me and tried to smile, but her eyes were elsewhere. I wanted to touch her, to comfort her, but felt my effort would be the weakest gesture. I didn't know how to help her. I didn't want to reach out and have her misconstrue my intentions. Perhaps the truth was I was in a state of shock myself.

Father, framed in the doorway, stood beside Mother. He raised his hands and waited for silence. Then he made an effort to meet the eyes of every individual in the room.

Finally he cleared his throat and spoke in a voice barely heard over the radio. "Our friend, our brother, Georgy Yakir, was murdered in the street. He was walking home, to be with Anna and Tanya and Natasha, when he was struck down by a car that did not stop, driven by a man who has not been, nor, I suspect, will be apprehended.

"The Soviet press did not and will not report this death. If it finds a reason to mention it, it will write that Georgy was on a treasonous mission, or was drunk, when he threw himself in front of a passing car."

He stopped and wiped his eyes, Mother took his arm. Tanya was stroking Natasha's hair while Anna sobbed, wringing a handkerchief in her lap.

Father continued. "One reason the Soviet press will not report Georgy's death is because it wants to erase the fact he ever existed. Georgy was the rarest of people: a brave man, unafraid of the state's brutality. Even after a harsh prison term, he continued compassionately to work for our cause. The authorities did everything in their awesome unchecked power to force Georgy either to submit or to leave the country in shame. He would not submit. He would leave here only as a free man. And I promise, they have not silenced him, even with his murder.

"His whole life, he was a teacher. His only goal was to help our young to think, to really consider the great issues of life. He succeeded beautifully with his daughter, Tanya, who has grown up to be a thoughtful young woman. Tanya, our hearts go out to you, your mother, and your sister."

81

"Thank you, Sergei," she whispered.

"The Soviets sent Georgy away to stop him from teaching," Father said. "To see him without a classroom was as sad as seeing a musician with a shattered violin. Yet he continued to teach by the example of his life. He taught us to love in a society where few know how. He demonstrated the meaning of freedom—freedom of thought in a land overburdened with restrictions. Like all gifted teachers, Georgy had the ability to make others ask questions they had long been afraid to consider.

"Even if the authorities are not directly responsible for his death, it is safe to assume they will shed no tears. They never despair at the death of a free-thinking individual. Besides, those tears of grief do not belong to strangers, they belong to us. We will never forget Georgy Yakir, our Georgy."

To no one but herself, Tanya whispered, "Goodbye, Daddy." Then she leaned against me, sobbing.

I looked around the room, but no one's eyes met mine.

12

Mother and I were sitting in a café, waiting for Father.

It was two weeks after Georgy's death. Two terrible weeks of frantic work while Father completed his history. I wanted to go away somewhere—as I suspect the others did. We were all on edge, and not only because of Georgy's death. There was a feeling that no one put into words, but it was there nonetheless.

Time was closing in. The apartment seemed more cramped than usual. Grandma lying on the couch, coughing. Ashtrays full of cigarette stubs. Father, unshaven, in the same shirt until he had started to stink. The smell of diesel oil in the air thicker, more suffocating. A rash of threatening letters—unsigned. Phone calls in the middle of the night—"wrong number." Pebbles thrown against the windows. Footsteps heard outside the door.

My parents kept me busy. I helped make meals for them and Malsa. I cleaned up. I watched Yulia. I played with her, and read the same stories over and over to her until I could recite them by heart. I knew the importance of the work being done in the other room and I was stuck watching my little sister.

From six in the morning till six at night, Father worked on the manuscript. When Mother came home, she wrote passages linking his documentation. And as soon as Malsa arrived, she would take off her coat, light a cigarette, and start to proofread. She hardly noticed me, except to request fresh tea or a washcloth to wipe her neck. Every night I put Yulia to bed, then sat listening to the Voice of America on the radio until I could no longer stay awake. When I went to bed, they were still working. The floor was littered with paper. Books open, face down. Scissors, pencils, clips. The finished pages stacked on a chair.

In the morning I'd wake Malsa, who had slept on the couch, using her coat as a blanket. She'd open her eyes and ask me to find her a cigarette. When Father went out for bread and cigarettes, Mother and Malsa went to their jobs. The agents across the street noted something in their book.

A few days earlier, we had found out that the Yakirs were leaving, allowed to emigrate to America, where they would live until they decided whether to continue on to Israel. Apparently, the authorities wanted the chapter of Georgy Yakir closed once and for all, performing the "humanitarian" act of allowing his widow and daughters to join relatives overseas. As much as I wished Tanya would stay, I knew it was best she left. What life would she have here? There were times I fantasized she would refuse to go, would stay with me, though I knew better. Tanya belonged with her mother and sister, not here.

I would miss her, desperately; my only solace was knowing that she would soon be safe and free in America.

Hers wasn't the only parting. Percy was also leaving the next day and had booked the same flight as the Yakirs', to make certain the authorities would not harass them. They wouldn't—not with an American journalist present.

Percy had arranged to meet Simon Reese in the morning, to hand over a microfilm copy of Father's history. Simon would send the microfilm to the West through the embassy's diplomatic pouch. Percy would pick up the microfilm in Washington, D.C., and bring it to Russian émigrés in New York City who would translate it into English. Within a week, Percy would begin a series of articles. We hoped his articles would create a stir in Washington. We knew the articles would most likely lead directly to Father's arrest.

Everyone was so calm, so accepting of the plan and its consequences. Everyone, that is, except for me. Of course, I knew we had to make plans, to keep the movement alive somehow, to have a meaningful result from Father's long years of work. But I knew I was witnessing the disintegration of my family. At times I couldn't—and still can't—help but hate my parents for allowing this to happen, though I knew they had no choice.

Mother ordered another cup of tea. "You're going to the Yakirs' from here, aren't you?"

"Yes."

She reached out her hand for mine. "I'm sorry it has to happen this way, Lev dear. I know we've ignored you of late. I'm sorry for that as well."

"Oh, I'm getting used to it."

She tightened her lips. "We have to stand up to them. Everyone's exhausted, not just you. Someone has to—"

"Go away?" I interrupted. "Die?"

"Lev, you're not the only one—"

"Who what? Who has a life he never asked for? Doesn't deserve? I don't want to hear about it, not now."

"Suit yourself." She clinked her fingernails against the glass.

We sat in silence until Father arrived. When he did, he took a seat next to Mother, facing me.

"Well?" Mother asked. I knew she meant the microfilm.

Father tapped his shirt pocket and winked.

"Now what?" I asked.

Father looked around. "Let's get out of here. We can talk as we walk."

Outside, I remembered the walks we used to take when I was younger. How our first walk each spring was a celebration of renewal, of the earth's awakening after another long winter. Now our walk had a different meaning. It was a slow mournful walk of parting, of farewell. We were removed from earth's rhythms, drawn inside our own world of separation and fear.

"So what about us?" I asked.

"We will continue our work," Father said, "though I don't know for how much longer. I suppose we've been left alone up until now because we're well known and many Westerners recognize our name and faces. But we also thought Georgy safe, that his association with us would somehow protect him. I guess we should have known better. Son, we must plan for the worst. I suspect the KGB will come for me as soon as Percy's articles are printed. That will be the final straw, as far as the KGB is concerned, but at least we will have played our last hand."

"Lev, if anything should happen to both of us, count

on Mochol Pevrod," Mother said. "She's a wonderful friend and knows the network in the event that you need something."

"What would happen to you?" I asked Mother.

"There's no telling," she said. "The important thing is to be prepared for any circumstance."

"You make it sound so easy! Well, I'm sorry, but I'm not always as clear-headed as you wish me to be. I have my own problems, you know. I . . ." I could feel the tears welling up in my eyes.

Father put his arm around me. "I know we've asked too much of you, Lev. But you're our son. You've made us proud in more ways than I could ever tell you. Mother and I aren't worried about ourselves. We're concerned for you and Yulia. Can we count on you to watch over her, to help Grandma around the house?"

"Do I have a choice?" I asked, wiping my nose.

"We can make other arrangements," Mother said flatly. "You can move in with Mochol."

"And live with all that dust?" I laughed, taking a deep breath. "You know you can count on me. I'll do what's right."

Father stopped. He took Mother and me in his arms, forming a tight little circle. I felt my parents' breath, their warmth. And they felt mine. I wondered if this would be the last time.

"I want to go say goodbye to Tanya," I said. "Will you tell Percy goodbye for me?"

"Of course," Father said. "I'm meeting him at his hotel in an hour."

"Tell him one day I'll come to America and he can take me to a rock concert."

"I'll tell him," Father said. He smiled. "Maybe we'll all go!"

Anna greeted me at the door with a hug and a kiss. "Tanya will be happy you came by. Will you help her while I look after Natasha?"

"Yes."

"Here, I have something for you." Anna picked up a coat from the sofa. I recognized it as Georgy's warm winter jacket. "I want you to have this."

I looked at the coat. I felt eerie, knowing it had been worn by a man who was now dead.

Anna realized I was uncomfortable. "It's a good coat, Lev. Please."

"Yes. Thank you. It looks very warm."

She leaned forward and kissed me on both cheeks, as Georgy used to.

Tanya was packing books into boxes as I entered the living room. She looked up and smiled.

"Lev!" She ran into my arms. It felt so good to hold her. We stood there close, rubbing each other's neck and back. Then, motioning to empty boxes on the ground, she started to tell me about how she'd been packing Georgy's books. "They'll be shipped later, after the censors make certain nothing important is leaving."

I knew neither of us wanted to say goodbye, but it had to be done. If things were not said then and there, they'd never be heard.

I looked around the room. There were light squares on the faded wallpaper where pictures had hung; scratch marks on the wooden floor where furniture had been removed; dust by the baseboards, previously hidden by a chair. The room lacked Georgy's good humor and Anna's touch. And I doubted if his ghost would ever want to return. All packed up, the room was empty of life, of memories, and could belong to anyone.

"I'll miss you terribly, Tanya," I told her.

"I'll miss you, too. Maybe in America someday . . ."

88

She sat on a box and started to cry. I went over and sat down next to her. She turned to me, her face puffy and streaked with tears, and offered me an embrace. We hugged each other tightly, knowing that embrace might have to last a lifetime. "I love you, Lev."

"And I . . . I love you. I can't believe you're leaving."

"We can write, and maybe someday we'll be together to stay."

Our arms around each other, we sat and wept, rocking our bodies together.

Anna walked in with Natasha. "Oh, I'm sorry to interrupt, but I have to get through to the kitchen."

We broke our embrace. Tanya wiped her face. I stood up and took a long, deep breath.

"I'd like to just sit here and be with you," Tanya said, "but you can see how much work we have left to do. Come on, I'll see you to the door."

"Goodbye, Anna," I called into the kitchen.

Anna came out, her arms extended. She gave me a long hug. "Goodbye, dear Lev. May only good things come to you."

"Tell Natasha goodbye for me." I didn't know what else to say.

Standing outside the door, I held Tanya tight. I knew I had to let her go but didn't want to, ever.

Across the street stood two men. Always the presence. Couldn't they leave us alone this once?

"It's not safe for you to be standing here," Tanya whispered.

"I don't care. I won't let you go."

"Don't let me go, Lev. Always hold me in your thoughts."

I was crying. "I will. I will."

She opened the door and started up the stairs. Then she stopped and turned around. She smiled as she wiped her eyes. "Take good care, Lev Kolokol. Shalom." She gave me her quick wave, as she always did when we parted, as if we'd see each other the next day.

I waved back and left.

Tuesday of the next week, newspapers from America, Canada, Great Britain, France, and West Germany were smuggled into Moscow, as they were each evening.

Every front page was devoted to the first in a series of articles by Percy Elliman, with excerpts from Father's history. There were pictures of my father, some taken years ago. And, of course, an angry denial by the Soviet authorities.

Staying up late to reread the article about Father over and over, trying to decipher every nuance in the Soviet message, I heard something I hadn't heard for a long time: my parents making love.

When, years earlier, I first realized what those strange sounds coming through their bedroom wall were, I was disgusted. They sounded so animal-like. But that night I felt different. Sure, I wished it was Tanya and me making those noises, sharing that closeness. But that was not to be.

Instead, I heard my parents sharing their last night together. And I felt no disgust—only warmth for those two special people behind the wall, for good people everywhere.

Later, that night, Father was taken away.

13

"Detonate!"

The blast was stronger than I expected. Standing too close, I had to cover my face with a coat sleeve to protect my eyes from falling debris. The sound reverberated in my ears.

"Boy, that was something!" I shouted, exhilarated by the explosion.

"It certainly was," Peter said. "I think we may have overdone it; but at least we know the formula works. We'd better get out of here."

Peter and I took off through the weeds, toward the bus stop and the bus that had taken us from the inner city to a vacant lot on the outskirts of Moscow.

I had spent a great deal of time with Peter since

Father's arrest. We spent most afternoons in his chemistry lab. The explosive we set off was homemade; Peter had let me do most of the preparations. If it weren't for his friendship, I can't imagine having made it through the months waiting for news of Father. Not that I came to confide in Peter; I still had to treat him with suspicion. But he had done nothing to raise distrust.

The vacant lot was full of garbage: broken glass and bricks, rusting cans. I had to jump over several piles of trash as we ran along.

I heard Peter fall and turned to help him back to his feet.

"What happened?"

"I was trying to keep up with you," he said, "and tripped over some loose stones." His shirt was badly torn, both his elbows bleeding. "What are we going to do?"

"Let's use your shirt for bandages; it's already ruined." When he took off the shirt, he started to shiver. "Here," I said, unbuttoning my coat, "take this. I'll be warm enough without it."

"What am I going to tell my parents?"

"Tell them we were climbing in the park and you slipped."

Peter put on my coat.

"Go ahead and keep it," I told him. "It doesn't fit me that well anyway. It belonged to Georgy Yakir. Anna gave it to me."

"I'm wearing a dead man's coat?" he said.

"What difference does it make? Would you rather catch a cold? Come on, if we're going to catch the bus, we'd better hurry."

Again we took off, running at full speed, dodging rocks and piles of trash.

When I got home I didn't share my afternoon with Mother or Grandma. They would only have yelled at me for doing something stupid. I knew it wasn't a smart thing to do: setting off a homemade explosive with Peter Simonov. But Peter had suggested it, and it had been exciting; a needed change of pace from the monotonous life at home without Father.

He had missed a lot in his absence, the little daily occurrences that make up family life. There were so many things I wanted him to know about, but after a while it was impossible to keep track of all the minute changes in our lives.

For the first two months after his arrest, I recorded the days without him on a calendar. At bedtime I crossed through another day. In the third month, I started to miss a day or two. By the fourth month I was crossing out weeks—when I thought of it. It was not that I didn't miss him; I did.

For those first months, every household ritual was marked by his absence: the empty place at the dinner table, the absent scent of his pipe, even the lack of his smell in the bathroom. I missed his calm reassurances that "everything will work out for the best"; his goodnight kiss; our walks and wrestling bouts. I missed having a man around.

No one could take Father's place at home, but I tried, at least symbolically. I took Mother to the cafés when I would rather have gone with Peter. I tried to mediate when Yulia was in a bad mood. As much as I could, I made a special effort to keep peace with Mother. It wasn't always easy. Some nights, when I thought I'd go crazy staying home, I agreed nonetheless to sit with Grandma and Yulia while Mother went to Mochol's for tea.

It got so tense at home that I started staying late at school to use the pool. After a couple of months, I had worked up to a kilometer without stopping. The exercise felt good. It was just me pushing my way through the water, giving my mind a chance to wander. Thoughts floated by. Going to America to see Tanya. Finding Father home one day. Having sex with Tanya. Winning the Olympics.

Mother and Grandma became agitated with me, I was spending so much time in the bathroom. But for the first time I was proud of my body: my muscles firm, shoulders wide. I had a sense of how I would look for the rest of my life. In the bathroom, studying the mirror, I was alone with my fantasies, away from what remained of my family.

I wondered whether, if I ever saw Father again, he'd recognize me.

I knew he was gone, yet I saw him everywhere.

On my way to school, I looked across the street and saw a man entering the bread shop. He was tall and strong like Father. He wore the same dark suit. Even the color of his thinning hair looked right. So I crossed the street and entered the shop. I pushed to the head of the long line. The women yelled and shoved me. "Wait your turn, boy, like everyone else."

"What do you want?" the woman behind the counter asked.

"A man just came in here," I told her. "Tall, with graying hair."

"That's our new baker, Myshkin."

"Can I see him, please?" I asked.

The woman called to the back. A man appeared, tying an apron behind him. He was not my father.

Late, I ran to school, and no sooner did class begin than I was called to the headmaster's office. Perhaps there was news of Father.

I left my desk. Walking down the hallway, I ran various possibilities through my mind: they had freed Father, apologizing that the whole thing was a horrible mistake. Or Father had confessed, telling them everything he knew in exchange for his freedom. Or he'd been found dead in his cell, a strip of bed sheet wrapped around his neck. Or they had killed him, but would report his death as a suicide. Or he had outsmarted them and escaped to the West, one day to bring the rest of us to freedom.

"Please sit down, Lev Kolokol," the headmaster instructed. I did as I was told, placing my hands on the wooden armrests of the large chair. "I have reports about your behavior which are quite disturbing."

"My behavior? I don't understand." I tried to be attentive, like everyone else, but there were times when I whispered something to Peter, or found myself looking out the window.

"Up until now you have been one of our most promising students," said the headmaster, "but recently your test scores have been below average. I suspect you are concerned about your father, and you are now living in a household of women, but this is no reason to let your studies collapse. Your father has committed crimes against the state, he is in prison awaiting a just trial; there is nothing you can do about that. To our credit, I believe, we have treated you like any other student. We are doing our part to educate you so you may one day contribute to our glorious revolution. I strongly suggest you do your part. You're dismissed, Kolokol."

I returned to class and tried to concentrate, to pretend nothing had happened. But everyone was looking at me. I felt as though someone had punched me in the chest, robbing my breath. How much longer would this continue? The icy stares? Being singled out by the teachers? Opening my notebook, I tried to involve myself with what was being discussed, but it seemed so unimportant. I couldn't stop my eyes from tearing, wetting my paper and causing the ink to blotch.

I walked a tightrope, trying to balance my family's beliefs with how I was expected to perform at school. I tried to keep my grades up, wanting the opportunity of attending the university, yet what I learned I was told at home to discard. I received two explanations—one at school, one at home—of how the world functioned. With Father gone, the distance separating the two worlds only widened.

Take history, for example. We studied Lenin's political philosophy until it was as familiar as the history of my own family was to me.

In class I read the questions on my exam:

> Lenin stated that imperialism is the highest stage of capitalism. Imperialism has three specific characteristics. Name them.

I remembered that Father had once told me Lenin's philosophy had been perverted by the current leadership, back to Stalin, for the sole purpose of consolidating its authority.

Mother said, "Every political system has a philosophical base, but that's not the whole truth. Certainly the American system is capitalistic, but that's only the economic truth. Socially and intellectually it is democratic. Free speech and debate are as much a part of the American system as capitalism is."

Yet, at school, capitalism was said to be responsible for the world's evil. Could both my parents and my teachers be right? Or wrong? Or not telling the whole truth?

To secure a good grade, I dutifully wrote:

> The characteristics of imperialism are: (1) monopoly capitalism; (2) parasitic, or decaying, capitalism; (3) moribund capitalism.

I was certain I had all the answers correct. But what would I gain? I was writing down lies to pass for truths, to secure respectability in a society I could never myself respect. And even if I received good grades, the authorities

96

knew who I was and would most likely prevent my advancement. At school I was supposed to be a cog in the great socialist revolution, trading my individuality for an assigned role among the masses. At home I was told of the honor of fighting for free speech and information, to work toward becoming a reflective and skeptical individual.

The tightrope grew thinner every day. And there was no safety net below me.

As the months passed, even my dreams changed. At first I dreamed of Father, often waking in fear at the moment when he was one scream away from being tortured to death. I never stayed asleep to witness his death; perhaps I could not accept this possibility. Certain images recurred: Father being given some powerful drugs. Father being tied to a chair and beaten. His eyes being poked. Father being left in a windowless cell for weeks.

One night, this dream took a strange twist. Father was strapped to a chair, about to be tortured, when suddenly his clothes were gone. Electrodes were attached to his testicles and a weak current was turned on. The charges coursed through his body. I felt a sensation of pain and excitement. Just before the dream broke, I looked at the face in the chair and it was mine; Father was now one of the torturers watching me. The current grew stronger, the tingling accelerated into quivering pulsations. I woke up and for a moment did not know where I was.

One reminder of Father's continued importance was the KGB agents who remained stationed across the street. They harassed any foreigner who came to visit us. Mother continued to meet Western journalists, imploring them to keep Father alive in the minds of those who could perhaps speed up his release. But, on reading the Western newspapers smuggled into Moscow, it became apparent that Father was no longer a major news story. Articles about him were pushed deep into the newspaper, no longer front-page material.

The KGB also followed us when we went out. Mother returned from the tailor shop where she worked, upset by the two agents who harassed her. Grandma and Yulia were watched at the playground. When the phone rang—which wasn't often, since they controlled our calls—everyone panicked. Mother and I would look at each other. I'd pick it up, but the result was always the same: no one was there. Packages were left outside our door, containing nothing but a lock of hair or a shred from a shirt—Father's? Late at night, when I got up to use the toilet, I'd pull the curtains back just enough to see men stationed across the street, the glow of cigarettes in the doorway. We were only one family. How many others were there enduring the same treatment?

No matter what pretense of family life was made—and Mother did her best—it was never real without Father. Perhaps if we had known he was dead we could have rebuilt our lives, created a unity of four instead of five. But we were kept in the dark. Our sole purpose, for all those months, was to obtain the smallest kernel of news about Father.

So one afternoon I stopped, as I always did, at the news vendor to buy a copy of the evening newspaper. Then I ran an errand I'd promised to do for Mother: picking up some aspirin for Grandma.

The clerk at the drugstore was surly, slamming my change down on the counter. Does he know who I am? Or does he act this way with everyone? Back on the street, I was elbowed by a man at a crosswalk. Was it an accident?

When I turned the corner on my block, I looked up at our windows to see the small plants Mother so carefully nurtured: a stroke of green in the otherwise dull building face.

Suddenly someone grabbed my arm and yanked me into a doorway. I hit the door with my back, and pain ran across my shoulders. I tried to move, but the way was blocked by three young men dressed in windbreakers. I didn't recognize them as I looked back and forth across their faces. One of them pushed my chest.

"So this is Lev Kolokol, the son of the scum traitor."

"I've seen your mother on the street," another said. "She looks lonely. I bet she'd like a real man for a quick one."

"Your grandmother likes her evening walk, doesn't she?"

The three of them talked at the same time, threatening to punch me in the face.

"First your father, then the rest of you."

"Your little sister has a sweet face—for now."

"I know everything you do, Kolokol, even when you play with yourself in the bathroom."

"What do you want?" I asked, my hands in front of my chest, palms exposed, fingers spread.

"You and your family don't deserve to live among good people."

"Are you members of the Komsomol?" I asked. "Is someone making you follow me? Why don't you just leave me alone?"

"You're the mindless, gutless son of traitors! No one tells us what to do."

"We'll be so close behind you, you better be careful when you scratch your ass that you don't poke us in the eye."

One of them punched me hard in the stomach. I lost my breath and doubled over. Someone—I didn't know which one—kicked at my knee. A blow to my temple forced me to my knees, and I pulled my arms into my body, trying to protect my ribs and face. I winced as I felt the impact of their boots against my body. Keeping my eyes closed, I tasted blood spilling from my nose.

When they ran off, I stayed doubled over, trying to catch my breath. I looked up at the people passing by. Some shook their heads, but no one stopped to help. I stood up and wiped the tears and blood from my face with my sleeve. My cheek felt puffy. The skin on my knuckles was shredded.

Without really considering why, I reached in my pocket to find the aspirin bottle. All I felt was broken glass.

I wondered why this brutality after all these months. My only thought was: They must be intensifying their harassment because Father's fate will soon be decided. His trial will be announced shortly.

And this was so. Within days of my being attacked, we read that the trial had been scheduled.

14

During Father's absence I pictured him many ways, trying to imagine his life in prison.

I saw him organizing the other prisoners, leading a successful hunger strike that resulted in more lenient treatment. I saw him hardening himself, waking to an hour of calisthenics, running around the confines of his cell. When I was reading my school assignments, I saw Father in the prison library poring over Soviet law books so he'd be in full command of the court's procedures. I fantasized he would beat the judge and procurator at their own game, outwit them. In my mind I saw him every possible way other than the way I found him the morning of his trial.

We were not informed of the date of Father's trial.

If Mochol had not brought over a copy of the international *Herald Tribune* published in Paris, the trial might have started without us.

At the foot of page 1 was the notice.

KOLOKOL TRIAL SET

Sergei Ivanovich Kolokol, well-known leader of the human-rights movement in the Soviet Union, will be brought to trial on Monday.

Mr. Kolokol was arrested last year for releasing a history of human-rights infractions by the Soviet government. He has been held incommunicado for 15 months at Lefortovo Prison in Moscow and is charged in a 40-page indictment with anti-Soviet agitation and propaganda. It is expected that the Soviet Procuracy will also charge Kolokol with treason for allegedly passing state secrets to foreign reporters.

Mr. Kolokol, through his wife, Irina, has repeatedly denied the charges alleged against him. If the trial fits the pattern of other dissidents', he may not be allowed to call any defense witnesses and Western press will not be allowed inside the courtroom.

A couple of weeks earlier, the same newspaper had carried word from America that two Soviet agents had been arrested in Washington and were about to go on trial for espionage charges. The two had been caught after buying information about a secret computer system from a man who turned out to be an FBI undercover agent.

We had hoped the authorities would schedule Father's trial soon, so, in the event the two Soviets were found guilty in America, the Kremlin might free Father in exchange for its spies. It had been done before: a dissident granted his freedom in trade for the release of convicted Soviet spies. I was certain Mother and Father would go along with such a deal, especially when the alternative was not having us together for many years, if ever again.

Monday morning, we got ready. It was important to have a record of the trial so the world would know how the proceedings were conducted. It was up to us to make such a transcript.

A full verbatim report of the trial was impossible. There would be no official tape recording or stenographic report made. The only official document would be made by the secretary of the court, containing the sequence of events and a small summary of the speeches. Afterward, the report would not be published, nor could anyone ever examine it in the office of the court. There would be a record, but it would be buried in the Soviet archives.

Without our report, the record of Soviet justice might never reach the outside world. And Father might be imprisoned or banished without a line of evidence about how it was done.

Mother and I would take notes when we could. And Mochol and Malsa would attend the court and take their own notes. We hoped that two people would be taking notes at all times, so the fullest report could be constructed afterward. There would be times when no one could take notes; still, we would do what we could.

Father was turned in his seat, looking at the gallery as we entered. He spotted us and started to stand. One of the two soldiers stationed beside him forced him back down. He did not resist.

After being frisked, Mother and I made our way to the front. Father pivoted in his seat to greet us; still sitting, he extended both his arms to Mother. She took his hands and started to lean over the barrier to kiss him. One of the soldiers started toward her and she moved back.

"Is it illegal to kiss one's husband?" she asked coldly.

Neither soldier responded.

"How are you, Sergei Ivanovich?"

He shrugged his shoulders. "I've been better," he said, attempting a grin.

I looked at this man, knowing that he was my father;

I recognized his look, yet so much else had changed. His face was pallid, as if he had spent months in a sickbed. His jowls were soft, his skin lined. He had lost much weight, his potbelly had vanished, yet his body did not look better for its disappearance. There was a slump to his spine, a slowness to his smallest movement—I had never seen him like this before.

The greatest change was in his eyes. Once they had been bright, alive with curiosity, shining. As I studied him, sorrow sprang up in my own eyes. Now, as I write about it, I realize I saw the look of a man who had grown familiar with his own insignificance. In his mind, Father must have traveled to his death and back many times in his isolation, because there was a hungry vacancy in his eyes that seemed to absorb all surrounding light while reflecting nothing. I looked deep into the black hollows of his pupils and saw only desolation.

What had he been through? What had they done to him? The man who, with my mother, had given me life, who had always been so robust, so powerful, who demanded everyone else live life to the fullest as he did—now he was apart from me. For the first time since his arrest, I admitted to myself that Father's chances for freedom were probably nonexistent.

"Hello, son," he said, looking around Mother.

"Father, are you well?" I said, my voice choking.

"It's been a long time, hasn't it?" was all he said.

"Sergei Ivanovich, all our friends are thinking of you. People around the world are praying for you," Mother told him. "We must not lose faith."

"Simple faith is something I moved beyond months ago," Father said quietly. "I now measure my life only in time."

"Yulia sends her love," I said, unable to say anything more important. "She's home with Grandma, who's feeling better of late."

104

He seemed to operate at the lowest possible levels. His mouth was slack, his breath shallow. His spent eyes reflected me back into myself. I felt I had done something wrong, had somehow brought a great disappointment to him. If only I had been a better son, if only I had not caused him shame—but for what, I did not know. For the past fifteen months we had kept the family together, functioning—yes, for ourselves, but also for him. I knew it was impossible, but couldn't he show us some love? Some gratitude? Somehow let us know the fight was worth its toll?

Of course I was well acquainted with how prison could break a person's spirit, reduce him or her to a creature concerned only with survival. But the last person I ever expected reduced to a being of total despair was my father. He had been so strong. They had taken him away from me and left a shell of a man. My father, once so solid; what would happen to me, to Mother, if they decided to send us away?

I was furious at their brutality and, somehow, furious with Father for not enduring. He knew we loved him. Couldn't that have sustained him? Weren't we reason enough not merely to survive but to resist them every moment he was away from us?

"I've tried to take care of things," I said, badly wanting him to know this.

"I knew you would, Lev," he said, closing his eyes.

I wanted to shake him, free him from whatever was troubling him. But I knew it was of no use; not now.

The courtroom seated between one hundred fifty and two hundred people. Father was seated in the middle, his back to the gallery. He faced a tall platform on which three chairs were positioned: one for the chairman of the court, the other two for the people's assessors, common Party members for whom it would be an honor to take part in court proceedings. Between Father's chair and the tribunal was a chair for witnesses. To Father's left was the secretary of the court, the procurator's table, and a chair for the state psychiatric expert. To Father's right was the defense table where his advocate would sit.

It was 9:45 when we were let in. Quickly every seat in the gallery was taken. Precisely at ten, the counsel for the defense, Konstantin Brushikin, who had—unsuccessfully—assisted other dissidents in the past, entered, followed by Procurator Akakievich, the psychiatric expert, and the secretary. Everyone took their seats.

The clerk shouted, "Rise, the court is in session!" Everyone stood. The side door opened and the tribunal entered. First one of the people's assessors, after her the chairman, Judge Yentzer, then the other assessor.

JUDGE: Be seated. I declare this session of the Moscow City Court Judicial Collegium for Criminal Cases open. Criminal case No. 937-18 will be held, in which Sergei Ivanovich Kolokol is being charged under Article 70, Paragraph 1, of the Russian Criminal Code, Article 72, and Article 190, Paragraphs 1 and 3. Kolokol, stand up.

[*Father slowly stood, pushing himself off the chair with both hands.*]

JUDGE: Kolokol, Sergei Ivanovich, born September 18, 1929. Is that your correct last name, first name, and patronymic?

FATHER: Yes, it is.

JUDGE: Russian, U.S.S.R. citizen, born in the city of Moscow, non–Party member, with higher education, married, no previous convictions, prior to his arrest unemployed, resident of Moscow. Is all that correct?

FATHER: I was trained as a mathematician. I suppose—

JUDGE: None of this "I suppose" business! Stand up straight! Look at the court! Now tell us, do you have a permanent job?

106

FATHER: I believe being a prisoner is full-time work.

JUDGE: We are not interested in your sarcasm. Have you received the indictment?

FATHER: Yes.

JUDGE: Do you have any petitions to the court at this time?

FATHER: I would like to know why I was arrested.

JUDGE: That is a question, not a petition.

FATHER: I do have a request. I want to know more about the people's assessors, where they work, whether they have taken part in court sessions before. I should like them to describe themselves. What are they getting out of this?

JUDGE [*Having consulted with the two assessors*]: They are office workers of Moscow. Yes, they have taken part in court sessions before.

FATHER: But what is their price for voting my fate? Did they get some meat or a better apartment? Perhaps a ticket to the ballet or a pair of sunglasses?

JUDGE: Kolokol, you will sit down.

[*Father sat down as the soldiers stepped toward him.*]

JUDGE: The court will proceed to the reading of the indictment. [*The judge opened a folder and began to read.*] On June 5 of last year, material containing fabrications defaming the Soviet political and social order was turned over to the Procuracy Office. The preliminary investigation established that the so-called Record of Human Rights Violations was written by Sergei Ivanovich Kolokol with the help of yet to be named fellow conspirators. This material was written for the purpose of duplication and distribution.

On June 6, several Western radio stations and newspapers announced the appearance in the West of Kolokol's material.

S. I. Kolokol used to meet foreigners frequently and maintained close relations with them. Matters of state security were often discussed in the presence of foreigners.

107

Confirmation of these charges is provided by items confiscated in the search of Kolokol's home.

On the basis of the above, Sergei Ivanovich Kolokol is charged with organizing group activities involving clear and treasonous disobedience to the legitimate demands of representatives of authority; with transmitting material to the West for publication; with circulating slanderous anti-Soviet literature in the U.S.S.R.; with deliberately compiling a collection of false statements derogatory to the Soviet state and social system; with agitation or propaganda carried out for the purpose of weakening or subverting the Soviet regime and of encouraging particularly dangerous crimes against the state.

Kolokol, you will rise. Is the meaning of the indictment clear to you?

FATHER: No, it is not clear.

JUDGE: What do you mean? You understand that you are being charged with anti-Soviet activities and treasonous acts?

FATHER: I understand that, but I do not understand the meaning of this indictment.

JUDGE: Nevertheless, if you understand the charges, do you plead guilty?

FATHER: No.

JUDGE: Be seated. The order of judicial investigation is as follows: interrogation of witnesses, the accused, and expert legal authorities if we deem such testimony necessary. The court will recess for one and a half hours so the assessors can acquaint themselves with the indictment. The accused shall remain seated. The gallery may clear if any so desire.

As the tribunal stood to leave, I had my first good look at the three people charged with determining Father's guilt or innocence.

Judge Yentzer was a stout, gray-haired woman in a gray suit. Her manner reminded me of a teacher I had last year who was more concerned with keeping order than instructing my class. Her hair was pulled into a tight bun behind her head. One eyebrow was constantly raised, as if in judgment. Her voice carried an offended tone.

The male assessor was young and looked as if he had competed in track and field events. He hardly looked as if he worked in an office, as the judge said he did. The female assessor had brown hair, streaked with gray. She had an unhappy look on her face, hardly sympathetic. She was probably Mother's age and she wore glasses perched on top of her long thin nose.

The hour and a half passed slowly. Mother and I did not leave our seats, knowing they'd be taken if we vacated them. I looked around the courtroom, not having been inside one before, trying to memorize everything, everyone. The faces were those of office workers: bland, pale. The seats were worn, the walls in need of paint. It was an undistinguished place in which to decide a man's fate.

When the tribunal returned, the judge called for the first witnesses, three KGB agents. I looked at Mother, who rubbed her forehead; this was the signal for me not to take notes. It was not worth the risk of getting stopped just to record these witnesses. Their testimony would no doubt offer no surprises and would appear in the evening papers.

So I sat and listened for the next four hours as the agents responded to the carefully planned line of questioning presented by Akakievich and the judge. "Evidence" was introduced. "Documentation" was offered. "Treasonous action" was outlined. Everything was orchestrated in an efficient manner.

A document listing the results of a search conducted at our home was read and entered into the trial report. I remember that day, four months after Father's arrest, when I came home from school to find three men looking through our belongings.

The search had begun in early afternoon. The men did not leave until well past nightfall. For hours, Yulia and Grandma had sat on the couch; Mother and I joined them when we got home. It was suggested that Mother voluntarily surrender any items pertaining to the investigation. She refused, so the men continued.

They were considerate of our things; still, I felt violated having them in our home, opening our drawers, picking through our books, looking in our closets and cupboards.

Large boxes were left in the living room and eventually filled as the men collected anything they felt could be of use. As the items dropped into the boxes, one man read the list aloud so we'd have an idea what was being taken:

> *Sheet of white paper with a note written in pencil starting with the words: "Radio broadcast," and ending with the words: "Information transformed into action."*
>
> *Piece of bent hollow copper tubing.*
>
> *Half-liter bottle containing congealed black dye.*
>
> *Carbon copies of typewritten text, size 12 x 18 cm; pages number 186–236.*
>
> *Novel by* V. Nabokov, Lolita, *Paris Russian-language edition.*
>
> *Sheet of paper with entry: "I was an anti-Party man," and ending: "Come on, let's take a hair of the dog."*
>
> *Standard sheet of white paper on which was noted "Moskva M-619, Kherson, d.7, kv.35, bus 101 to Khersonskaya St."*

The boxes were filled and then sealed with heavy tape and labeled. At one point, one man used our phone— it was working—to call and request more boxes. He thought this was amusing.

In my mind I searched my room, trying to remember what, if anything, I might have that would be taken. I mentally panned like a camera: across the shelves, into the closet, through the drawers, under the bed. I did this several times and came up with nothing. But one of the men stayed in my room for a long time and I grew anxious.

Finally he emerged, but only to call to the others, "Come and have a look at this!"

Then I realized what had happened.

I got up from my chair.

"Lev, where are you going?" Mother shouted. "Stay here."

But I was already in my doorway before she finished.

There, sitting on Yulia's bed, I saw them: uttering crude remarks, elbowing one another, leering over the magazine Percy had given me. I had forgotten it had remained under my mattress for months. How could I have been so stupid!

"That's mine," I said and started toward them.

One of the men stood and put out his arms to stop me. "This is official business, Lev Kolokol."

"These American women are both healthy and friendly," another said, opening the centerfold and rotating the magazine.

"They are all whores," the third man said. "They are sluts who display the corruption of Western morality."

There was nothing to do, so I started back to the living room.

"Wait. I have something else to show you." One of the men reached into his pocket and handed me a slip of paper. "I found this tucked inside one of your schoolbooks."

It was the formula Peter had given me for making gunpowder.

"We will turn this over to our scientists," he said.

111

"If it's what I think it is, you are in very big trouble. Chances are, though, if you behave yourself we will remain silent about the pornographic material you have smuggled into Moscow. Be a good boy and we will consider safeguarding the formula and the magazine—if you keep your mouth shut."

I was dumfounded. The only thoughts I had were: I must want to be caught. Why else would I be so stupid as to keep these things in my room? Why did I set myself up to hurt my parents and punish myself? When would I act responsibly? When would I grow up?

I waited, ready to rush from the courtroom in shame when the magazine and formula were announced. I listened anxiously, suffering a tense feeling of nausea, as the list of confiscated material reached its end. To my relief, I was spared. Perhaps the KGB agents were keeping their word.

The trial's first day came to an end as the judge declared the court adjourned at 21:30 hours. Witness after witness had testified they were eyewitnesses to my father's treachery. Akakievich delivered people who claimed they knew Father during his college days when he organized anti-patriotic rallies. One said she had broken off an engagement to my father when she discovered he was distributing anti-Soviet literature. One man, whom I had never seen, reported that Father had "confided" in him plans to "subvert our glorious revolution." A young woman swore Father had promised her money if she turned over official prison documents to him.

These were all lies, and I sat in angry silence, unable to denounce any of the testimony. There was nothing I could do to prevent this slander from becoming more factual than the truth, which would never be heard.

Father was helped from his chair by two soldiers and led away. Mother and I were both drained, unable to reach him before he left. We called out to him, but couldn't be heard above the noise of chairs being moved and the shouts of the crowd calling for Father's punishment.

Before he disappeared through the doorway, Father turned in our direction and gave a twist of his head, as if to say, "And what could we have expected from a Soviet court?"

15

After Mother and I were taken aside and quickly frisked, we entered the courtroom for the second day; Malsa was not there.

She had sat several rows behind us the day before, taking notes as we were doing. But that night neither she nor Mochol stopped by and dropped off their notes. It was too late for anyone connected with Father to be on the streets.

The evening newspapers, which I clipped and hid, carried full coverage: articles, opinions, even letters to the editors, which had miraculously been written, delivered, edited, and printed before the court was adjourned. From an editorial in *Vechernaya Moskva*:

> There is an uproar among the sensation-seeking, anti-Soviet propagandists of the foreign gutter press, the

commentators of Voice of America, and all the rest. All the stops have been pulled out to release howls about freedom, of which we, dear readers, are evidently being deprived.

These "concerned observers of human rights" are firmly convinced that crude summary justice will be meted out in Moscow to a so-called writer, a self-appointed authority and fighter for his fellow Soviet citizens. A man whose name means absolutely nothing to the Soviet reader, since to this day he cannot be credited with a single published line.

Who is this man brought to trial?

S. I. Kolokol, over fifty and still without a fixed occupation. He was dismissed from his last position as a college instructor for reasons too numerous to list here. Since then he has become a parasite accused of having criminal ties with the disseminators of slanderous anti-Soviet propaganda.

No clear-thinking citizen will be duped by the hypocrisy of this slanderer and of those who clumsily try to shield and defend him.

From *Izvestia*:

I fought in the Great Patriotic War and was gravely wounded. How can I fail to feel renewed pain when a vile and ungrateful creature slanders me and all the Soviet people?

The Soviet court must punish the slanderer! He should be branded with shame as a lackey of the enemies of our people.

I. Vischagin, Kalinin State Farm

This is the first letter we have written to your paper. We cannot find words to express our indignation at the anti-Soviet activities of S. I. Kolokol. We are seething with rage that people nurtured by the Soviet system, instead of showing their gratitude, can spit on the soul of our people and betray us. S. I. Kolokol is not a man, he is worse than the typhus louse. Soviet people know that lice are dangerous and spread disease, and that is why we render them harmless.

We hope the court passes a just sentence, and this parasite is made to serve his term to the end. By unremitting physical labor he might atone in a small way for his great guilt before our people.

Students of the B. M. Kisov Institute
of Biological Technology

We all stayed up late, unable to sleep, listening to classical music on the phonograph. None of us had much to say.

I had tossed in bed for hours, too many thoughts preventing my sleep. I tried to devise ways to help Father, but every idea hit a snag, and I felt helpless.

[*After hearing the last of Procurator Akakievich's witnesses, the judge motioned to Father.*]

JUDGE: Kolokol, stand up and come here. Have you any questions pertaining to the charges?

FATHER: First of all, I want to say I view myself as an ordinary person. May I begin by reminding the court of words spoken by Lenin in 1903, "We demand immediate and unconditional recognition by the authorities of freedom of assembly, freedom of the press, and an amnesty for all 'political' prisoners and dissenters. Until freedom of assembly, of speech, and of the press is declared, there will not disappear the shameful Russian inquisition which persecutes the profession of unofficial faith, unofficial opinions, unofficial doctrines."

[*"Silence the parasite!" a man shouted from the gallery. "He deserves no justice," a woman added. "Sentence him now!"*]

FATHER: My fellow citizens in attendance are free to express their opinions—

JUDGE: I allowed you a question, not a rebuttal to loyal citizens whose indignation is duly noted by this court.

FATHER: As you insist. The court speaks of justice. How am I to expect justice when I have been kept in strict isolation for fifteen months, and then given only three days in which to examine over sixty volumes of investigative material collected during my detention? How can I expect a fair judgment when the tribunal spent only a few hours discussing these volumes? How—

116

JUDGE: Kolokol, you will sit down!

[*When Father did not move, two soldiers approached him and took him back to his chair.*]

JUDGE: Does the defense have any questions?

BRUSHIKIN: I'd like to call witnesses to testify on behalf of S. I. Kolokol: his wife, his former colleagues from the university.

JUDGE: I asked for questions. If you have a petition, present it to the court and we will consider it.

[*Konstantin Brushikin, counsel for the defense, approached the tribunal and handed over his written petition.*]

JUDGE: Court will recess for an hour, at which time we shall respond to this petition.

During the recess Father turned toward me and mouthed the question: "Where's Malsa?"

I shrugged my shoulders, then asked Mother.

"How should I know?" she said.

"Do you think something happened to her?"

"It's possible, anything is possible," she said, "but she's a grown woman and has taken good care of herself in the past."

"Isn't there anything Brushikin can do to help Father?" I asked. Brushikin had followed the proceedings carefully, taking notes he would attempt to enter in the official report. But he had rarely questioned any of the judge's rulings. He'd asked only superficial questions to the string of witnesses for the procurator.

"Konstantin is doing all he can," Mother said. "If he upsets the court, he might face expulsion from the Lawyers' Union and then he wouldn't be any good to us. He is a good man, but always practical."

"So we'll just sit and watch them convict Father?"

"Lev, this is the opening round. The real fight will come

117

afterward when we must get the West to intercede on our behalf."

We stayed in our seats while people moved in and out of the courtroom. The mood in the gallery was buoyant, people were talking loudly and joking. The crowd was loyal to the Soviet leadership and I felt as if I were attending a sporting event. It was difficult just to sit there, so I took out a piece of paper and started a letter to Tanya.

On three occasions before Father's trial, friends of the movement brought me letters from her. She referred to letters I never received, so she must have written often.

America was agreeing with her. She had taken extra classes at night to improve her English. Her gymnastic skill made her popular at school. She was so good she helped teach the younger girls. Her mother had found a job in a small printing shop. They had an enormous apartment, a color television set, and two radios. Neighbors had been very kind, bringing over hot meals and extra clothing.

I had written back several times. I wrote her things I could never say to her when she was here. I took time with my letters, often rewriting them several times, trying various salutations and signatures. She never acknowledged receiving any of them, but I felt a need to reach out to someone.

> Dear Tanya:
> As I write, I am sitting in court at Father's trial. I'm sure you will read the results long before this letter reaches you—if it does—and the verdict will come as no surprise. I guess you knew much more all along how things work here. School is fine. Guess what? I started to train for swimming. Maybe someday we'll meet at some international sports event. I think of you, dream of you, but I guess you've met a lot of nice Brooklyn boys by now . . .

"Lev, put that paper away!" Mother said, grabbing the pencil from my hand.

118

"It's only a letter to Tanya," I tried to explain.

"You have other times to write her. There are dozens of agents in this room with orders to throw us out if they catch us writing anything. How could you be so stupid?"

I looked at her and ripped the letter to shreds. "Satisfied?"

Mother took a deep breath, turned her head away from me, and started to rub her arm. She had nothing to say.

JUDGE: The court denies the defense counsel's petition. Malsa Isakov, please come forward and tell the court the facts you know about this case.

[*Father turned around and started to speak, but the soldiers moved toward him. Mother stared straight ahead, the muscles in her neck suddenly taut. At the back of the courtroom the door opened and Malsa entered. Both of her hands were bandaged. She looked as if she had not slept, and her hair was disheveled. Keeping her head down, she walked directly to the witness area. Turning to face Father and the gallery, she then sat down, aided by one of the soldiers.*]

JUDGE: Tell us how you became acquainted with the defendant.

MALSA: Sergei was my—

JUDGE: Speak up! Everyone wants to hear you.

MALSA: He was my instructor at the university. I have known him for some years now. Our meeting was chance, but we became friendly.

AKAKIEVICH: This friendship was not linked with any activity?

MALSA: No.

JUDGE: Tell us how you helped Kolokol prepare his material.

MALSA: What?

JUDGE: You heard me. What did you do for Kolokol?

MALSA: I helped him with some of his proofreading,

that's all. From time to time, he asked me to help with typing or editing. And I baby-sat his two children when he and his wife went out.

AKAKIEVICH: Were you aware of the anti-Soviet nature of the material?

MALSA: I didn't know the content.

JUDGE: You just said you helped proofread. You didn't know what was written?

MALSA: Yes, I suppose I did. But it was some time ago . . .

AKAKIEVICH: Did you receive payment for your help?

MALSA: No. I did it out of friendship.

AKAKIEVICH: To whom did Kolokol pass his material?

MALSA: I don't know. He and I never talked about it specifically.

JUDGE: Do you deny the anti-Soviet nature of Kolokol's material?

MALSA: What?

AKAKIEVICH: You heard the judge's question. Answer it.

MALSA: There were a great number of projects I helped him with. I can't specifically recall what anything was . . .

AKAKIEVICH: Need I remind the witness of the charges she herself faces if her memory continues to fail her?

JUDGE: Why did you assist in the preparation of anti-Soviet propaganda?

MALSA: I . . . I . . .

AKAKIEVICH: Did Kolokol ask you to type some letters in code?

MALSA: I typed one copy of a letter on tissue paper in his apartment. There were some figures. I think M-619, 7, 35, 101 were among the figures.

JUDGE: And you didn't ask Kolokol what they meant?

MALSA: No.

AKAKIEVICH: Did he himself ask you to type this letter?

MALSA: Yes, I typed it in his presence.

JUDGE: Do you admit that you are guilty of anti-Soviet activity?

120

MALSA [*Sitting in silence for a short while, looking at her bandaged hands, then whispering*]: Yes.

AKAKIEVICH: Speak up!

MALSA: Yes. YES!

[*A spasm ran up my back. I took a quick breath. I started to sweat.*]

JUDGE: How do you regard your activity?

MALSA: With shame.

AKAKIEVICH: How will you live in the future?

MALSA: Differently.

JUDGE: Do you intend to renounce this activity?

MALSA: Yes, yes, I do intend to.

AKAKIEVICH: May we expect you to live as an honorable citizen of the Soviet Union?

[*Malsa looked at Father with tears running down her cheeks. Father motioned to his defense counsel, Brushikin, who came over to confer with him.*]

MALSA: I said I intend to renounce this activity.

JUDGE: Defense, do you have any questions?

BRUSHIKIN: Malsa, tell me, please, what kind of relations existed between you and S. I. Kolokol?

[*Malsa looked at Father with a shocked expression, as if she could not understand the question.*]

MALSA: We were friends.

BRUSHIKIN: Didn't you have many conversations with Kolokol in which you expressed affection? Haven't you told him repeatedly that you love him?

[*Malsa lowered her head.*]

FATHER [*Shouting*]: Answer the question, Malsa Isakov!

MALSA: Yes, I said such things.

BRUSHIKIN: Can we assume that you worked with him because you love him?

MALSA: Assume what you want.

BRUSHIKIN: Didn't he take you into his home? Didn't you break bread with his family many evenings?

MALSA: Yes. Yes. YES! [*She wiped her eyes. Her nose was*

121

dripping.] Sergei Ivanovich, why are you doing this? You know our relationship means nothing to them. Why stir up ugly gossip? Why destroy—

FATHER [*Interrupting her, shouting*]: Did we not have an affair? And didn't you assist me because you were afraid you'd lose my love if you didn't help?

MALSA: No! . . . I mean, yes, we . . . yes, we had an affair. But no! I helped you because . . . I knew from the start I couldn't keep you.

BRUSHIKIN: I petition the court to disregard the testimony of this witness. She is obviously still emotionally involved with the defendant and her testimony should not be considered. She is an intelligent but confused young woman. The court should realize her testimony is a desperate attempt to defame him. This is a jealous, ungrateful woman who—

JUDGE: Defense, take your seat. Kolokol, restrain yourself or I'll have you removed. There is no reason to harass a witness who came forward with important information.

MALSA: Sergei Ivanovich, I . . . I . . . [*She looked up, finding Mother and me in the gallery.*] Irina, Lev, you must . . .

JUDGE: Take the witness away. Escort her out.

MALSA: I would like to remain present in court.

JUDGE: There is no room in the courtroom. We can't allow you to stay.

MALSA: I can stand.

JUDGE: No, you must go.

[*A soldier approached and took Malsa's arm. Her face was slack, bloated by crying. Her head swayed as if she was having difficulty breathing. She held her bandaged hands across her chest as the soldier helped her to her feet. Father slumped in his chair, staring at the floor. I looked at Mother. Her head was back, her chin up, eyes closed as she struggled to maintain control.*]

JUDGE: This session is declared adjourned until tomorrow

122

at ten hundred hours. Tomorrow we shall call on the procurator and defense counsel for their statements. Our verdict will follow.

We never expected Father would simply be forgiven and released; he was much too important a figure to be branded a "parasite" and freed with his shame. But I never expected one of our inner circle—Malsa—to betray us. Nor had I expected to see Father turn on her as he did. They had taken away our home, our happiness; now they were after our foundation of trusted and loyal friends.

I felt so isolated, so vulnerable, in my shrinking circle. I reached over and took Mother's hand, held it while the people around us cleared out. "Come on," I finally said, "let's go home."

Outside the courthouse, Mother was detained by a foreign journalist wanting an account of the day's proceedings. She was in no mood to talk—words, at times, serve no function—but realizing she was the only source the reporter had, she stayed.

Soon some men came and disrupted the interview, informing the journalist he'd face arrest if he continued to talk to Mother. Mochol Pevrod pushed her way through the men.

"Come on, Irina," she said, "I'll walk you home."

I knew I should go with them, but I had to be alone, to walk and let the day's events float in my mind until, I hoped, they settled into sense. At the corner I turned away from Mother and Mochol.

"Lev, where are you going?"

"I can't go home, not yet. I need to be alone."

"Come back here," Mother shouted.

"No!"

"Irina, the boy can take care of himself," Mochol said. "Lev, be home soon."

"I just need some time to myself."

"Lev, you're all I have. Just you and Grandma and Yulia and Mochol. I . . . Please be careful, son."

Down the streets I went, followed by two agents, past people who wouldn't meet my glance. I picked out as many passersby as I could, boring into their eyes with mine, trying to loosen an image of a people who would stand by and let them take Father away, but was met by their aversion.

I walked to the bank of the Moskva River, southwest of the Kremlin. The water below, which had flowed during centuries of authoritarian regimes, war, glory, poverty, and revolution, looked inviting in its swiftness.

End this. Carry me away, I thought. The water so free. What's the use? What future would I have other than endless harassment? What hope? It'd be so easy to strike the chilly surface, plunge under, and be lost in the free currents; to be pushed down with Father, Mother, Malsa, my confusion, no sense of a future. Endless. Alone. Hopeless.

The Kremlin walls loomed at my back. The agents stood nearby, perhaps hoping I would jump so they could go home and be rid of me. It'd be so easy. One moment to gather what strength remained, the next moment to be gone. Finished. Free. I can't make a difference. Go ahead. Jump. Be done with it.

I leaned over the stone barrier. My head felt light, the attraction of the swift water was a relief from the weight of the city. I spotted a stillness in the murky gray water and concentrated on that area. There was a calm eye in the river around which swirled eddies moving in contradiction to the powerful main current.

My eyes stared at the calm eye, finally seeing a vision of their own. Concentric circles spun around the eye, against the river's power. The circles revolved faster and

124

faster, creating a small whirlpool in the middle of Moscow. Water reeled round and round in a central vortex that grew in strength until I thought I could see the bottom of all things submerged deep in consciousness.

At last I blinked, clearing the vision. I drew my finger to my eyes and wiped away tears that dropped into the river. My tears merged with the river of Moscow's being, to begin a journey to the great free oceans of the world.

Then I thought, this is what's important: the flow of nature, of time. I am a part of this. The manmade world of fear and threats, politics and repression, would be long gone or replaced before the river would stop its path through the earth.

I was right, I don't make a difference—unless I decide to. Besides my tears, the river had engulfed other human lives: blood and waste, carrion disposed by the state, lost wedding rings, birthstones. Yet it never halted, overburdened by sadness; it continued to flow, to sustain its own life.

Without understanding why, I felt a sudden clear vision of being forgiven—and forgiving. Father was still a person to love and admire, as was Mother, for all their faults. And so was I.

I walked alongside the river into the innermost rings of the city. Leaving the water, I returned to the urban world and soon found myself in Dzerzhinsky Square— which is actually circular-shaped—named after a Soviet revolutionary leader. Needing a rest, I sat down facing the KGB building at 2 Dzerzhinsky Square. The autumn chill did not bother me, as I was still warm from my long walk.

I watched people come and go from the KGB building. No one looked recognizable until I saw someone I had neither the expectation nor the desire ever to see again: Malsa Isakov.

As she left the building, she crossed the square. Obviously nervous, she constantly looked behind her. I figured she was going to the bus stop on Kirov Street. Then she spotted me and stopped. I made no effort to signal her, keeping my hands in my pockets. She must have run excuses through her mind as to why she should not approach me, because it was nearly a minute before she moved again, toward me.

"Hello, Lev," she said.

"Visiting your friends at the KGB?"

"I was ordered to report after the trial," she said.

I looked at her but said nothing.

"You have to believe I meant your father no harm."

"Sure," I said. "You were helping him, weren't you?"

"No," she said quietly, ashamed. "I did not help him." She extended one of her bandaged hands toward me. I shifted my shoulder away. "Can we take a walk?"

"What for?"

"So I can tell you what happened."

"I was there," I said. "I saw what happened, Malsa Isakov."

"Please, Lev, can we walk, away from here? I'm afraid we're being watched."

"What's the matter? Afraid your buddies at the KGB might see you with me? What difference would it make? I imagine they're quite pleased with your performance."

"I suppose they are," she said, not wanting to start an argument. "Please, let me explain. I could get arrested just for talking to you, you know that. But it's important you know why I said the things I did in court. I want you and your family to realize what they did to me."

"How about what you did to us! We trusted you." I knew it wasn't just Malsa who had betrayed me, who had disappointed me. But Malsa was the one present, and deservedly or not, she would have to explain. "So go ahead,

126

tell me why tomorrow my father will be sent away, why the Yakirs are gone forever, why the Kremlin can snap into pieces the integrity of its citizens. I'm listening."

She looked at me, trying to gather her thoughts. I stood and started to walk. "Are you coming?" I asked.

Her eyes remained fixed on the ground as she started to talk, "After yesterday's session I was met at my apartment by two agents. They told me they knew I was making a record of the trial and said they had a long list of allegations against me. They said I must cooperate and give testimony against Sergei Ivanovich, or face the consequences. I refused." She threw back her head to clear the hair from her face. "Last night, I found out what those consequences were. In the middle of the night I was awakened by the sound of men running down the street. I got out of bed and put on a robe. I felt something was wrong, then I smelled smoke outside my door. A pile of trash was in flames in the hallway. I knocked on my neighbors' door, allowing them to make their escape. Then I tried to extinguish the fire, but ended up only burning my hands. Firemen arrived after a thirty-minute delay, along with an investigator, who immediately charged me under Article 150."

"Article 150? What's that?" I asked.

" 'Negligent destruction or damaging of the personal property of citizens.' The damage to the building was estimated at 2,500 rubles. And the investigator searched my room, finding some papers he said were 'of an illegal nature.' It must have been four in the morning before I was taken to Procurator Akakievich's office. There I finally received treatment for my burns. Akakievich told me the options. I could either cooperate and admit in court I helped prepare Sergei's material, or face the maximum sentence under Article 150: two years' deprivation of freedom and a large fine. Akakievich was very persuasive, saying Sergei's defense did not have a chance, that my testimony would only supplement that of other witnesses."

"Does that mean you had to go along with them?" I asked.

"Lev, what choice did I have? Sergei understands. I'm sure he does."

"Well, I don't! Why'd you get involved at all if you weren't willing to face the consequences?"

"Try to understand," she said quietly. "Those of us around your father felt he'd somehow protect us, that he was too important ever to be arrested. Of course I agreed with the political and moral reasons behind the human-rights movement. But I committed myself more out of . . . well, admiration for your father, not specifically on some theoretical belief in the movement." She placed her arm over mine; I didn't move it away.

"Why did you and Father get involved?"

"He's a very attractive man, and . . . these things happen. We spent a great deal of time together, your father and I. They were exciting times. We were under constant pressure and knew we might be stopped from completing the history at any time. It was exhilarating. I make no apologies for what I did."

"And what about my mother? Did you ever think of her?"

"Of course, of course." Malsa forced me around so I had to look at her. "Lev, this may not be easy for you to hear, but your parents' marriage has become more of an agreement of late than anything else."

"What's that supposed to mean?"

"I mean, your parents were together because they shared their work. They stayed together for you and Yulia. But, as people, they had little in common any more. I think they acknowledged this to each other—if not to you."

I raised my hand to my brow, hoping to stop the rush of tears I felt starting. "What am I going to do?" I moaned. "What am I going to do?"

"What can any of us do?" Malsa whispered as if only speaking to herself. And then she took me and hugged and rocked me in her arms.

16

In the morning I shaved, using Father's razor. I had been using it since he left. Mother never said anything about getting my own; perhaps she thought I still didn't need one.

After breakfast, Mother and I boarded a bus to the courthouse. For the first time, reporters were allowed to gather inside and they bombarded us with questions. Mother and I moved past them, not stopping to talk.

We climbed the stairs to the courtroom, and at the top, where we were usually frisked, I was met by a soldier who ordered me to return to the main floor and report to a room and wait to be searched.

"Better do as he says," Mother said. "I'll save you a seat."

"But the trial is set to start in ten minutes," I said.

"They know this," she said.

The room was equipped with only two chairs. There were no windows; the walls were bare. I was too edgy to sit, so I leaned against the wall. I tried to keep track of the time, and it must have been nearly an hour before a soldier finally appeared.

"Empty your pockets," he said.

I put everything on the seat of a chair: my keys, some change, wallet, pencil, and small squares of paper.

"What's this for?" the soldier asked, indicating the pencil and paper.

I shrugged my shoulders.

He picked up everything from the seat and started for the door.

"Where are you going?" I asked.

"I have to bring this to my supervisor."

"But the trial has already started."

"I have my orders," he said, then added sarcastically, "Don't worry, Kolokol, I'll try to hurry."

When he left, I tried the door. It was locked.

It was such a long time before he showed up again that my legs grew tired and I had to sit down. Two floors above me the final statements in Father's trial were going on, and I was not there to witness the proceedings. The authorities were toying with me, humiliating me. I hated them for their pettiness. What difference did I make?

When the soldier returned, he was accompanied by two other men. I did not get up when they entered.

"Stand up," the soldier said. "Stand up!"

I did as he instructed.

"Now take off your shoes."

"My shoes?"

"You heard me. Or are you deaf? Come on, you're the one in the hurry. Don't question my authority."

Steadying myself with one hand on the chair, I removed first one shoe, then the other.

"Hand them to me."

I picked up the shoes and gave them to the soldier. He gave one each to the two men, who examined the shoes, testing the heels and pulling out the inner soles.

"Now your socks."

"Are you serious?"

"The socks!"

I pulled them off and handed one each to the men.

"Your coat and shirt. Hand them over."

It was cold in the room, so I crossed my arms to try to keep warm. I stood in the middle of the room, under a single light bulb that dangled from a wire.

The men picked up my things and left without a word.

I walked around the room, trying to keep my feet warm. When I heard the door being unlocked, I moved to the far wall.

The three men entered smiling, as if just having heard a joke. But when the soldier looked at me, his expression changed.

"Everything else off. Pants and underwear."

I moved my hands to my belt. "What for?" I asked. My heart began to accelerate, sweat started in my armpits. "I have nothing there."

The men laughed. "I'm sure you have nothing there," the soldier said. Again his expression changed suddenly. "Take them off. Or we will."

I unbelted my trousers and pulled down the zipper. I sucked in my belly and put my thumbs inside the waist. In one motion I pulled my pants and underwear down to my ankles and nearly fell over trying to step out of them. It was as if I had never been naked before, I felt so vulnerable.

"Give them to me. Give me the pants."

I handed them to the soldier, who went through the

pants pockets. Then he took the underwear, held it high above his head, and with his free hand squeezed his nose as if suppressing a horrendous smell. The other men laughed at his action.

"Now what?" I asked, holding my hands in front of me. "You're not going to leave me like this, are you?"

"Would we do such a thing?" the soldier asked. "Come here. Stand before me."

I moved to him. He ran his fingers harshly through my hair. "You're hurting me," I shouted.

"Good. I like it that way." He pulled open my mouth. "Nothing hiding in there," he reported. Then he took my arm and yanked me toward the chairs.

He sat down in one of the chairs, still holding my arm. "Lie, stomach down, over the other chair," he ordered.

"What?" I tried to pull away. "You have no right—"

"Don't tell me what to do," he shouted. He pulled me down, forcing me across the chair. Before I could move, the other men took hold of me. One took my arms, the other my feet. They pulled hard, stretching me flat against the hard seat.

"Now!" the soldier said. And the man at my feet spread my legs. The soldier quickly stood up and lifted the chair over me, lowering it between my knees. Then he stepped over my leg and sat down. He forced his knees against the inside of my thighs, spreading them wider.

"Now then, let's see what you're hiding in there."

When they finished with me, I dressed as quickly as I could and rushed upstairs to the courtroom. The gallery was full, so I stood just inside the door to hear the judge proclaim, "Sergei Ivanovich Kolokol is found guilty of contravening Article 70, Paragraph 1, of the Russian Criminal Code, Article 72, Article 190, Paragraphs 1 and 3, and is sentenced as follows: under Article 70, Paragraph 1, to seven years' deprivation of freedom in a strict-regime corrective labor colony, with an additional term of five years' exile; under Article 72, to seven years' deprivation of freedom in a strict-regime corrective labor colony, with an additional term of five years' exile; under Article 190, Paragraphs 1 and 3, to three years' deprivation of freedom in a strict-regime corrective labor colony, and a fine of 100 rubles. The terms of imprisonment will begin today. The prisoner will be led out. Court is adjourned."

There was stormy, prolonged applause in the gallery as I added up Father's sentence: seventeen years in a work camp followed by ten years internal exile.

When I forced my way to the front, Mother was talking to Konstantin Brushikin. "Irina," he was saying, "we have seven days to appeal the sentence to the Supreme Court. We still have a chance."

"No," Mother said. "Konstantin, you are a decent man. Go home to your family. Sergei Ivanovich's fate now lies in the hands of the West. It is our job, not yours, to make certain they care enough to save him."

As we left the courthouse, there were two men taking photographs of everyone who had attended the trial. No doubt they were KGB agents, for when a foreign journalist attempted to take our picture he was quickly surrounded by agents in civilian clothes who told him to leave immediately.

I must have been in shock, because it finally came to me that neither Mother nor I had had a chance to say goodbye to Father.

17

SPY SWAP SOUGHT FOR KREMLIN CRITIC
by Percy Elliman

A high-ranking Administration official stated today that the White House is interested in the case of Russian dissident Sergei Ivanovich Kolokol.

Kolokol, who has been a thorn in the side of the Soviet leadership because of his active role in the human-rights movement, was sentenced to seventeen years in a labor colony, to be followed by ten years' internal exile. After a brief trial in Moscow, Kolokol was found guilty of "treasonous acts and anti-Soviet propaganda and agitation" and other charges.

Despite his many brushes with the authorities in the past, Mr. Kolokol was regarded as almost immune to prosecution because of his international standing. His trial and conviction are a serious blow to proponents of human rights in the Soviet Union.

The fact that the Soviet authorities moved against

him at this time seems to reflect the dramatic deterioration of relations with the West. Apparently the Kremlin felt it had little to lose by silencing one of its foremost critics. Furthermore, the Kremlin leadership has suffered few international repercussions by not adhering to recent agreements regarding the loosening of restrictions on travel and democratic activities.

The White House said the United States would welcome the activist just as it had welcomed other Soviet dissidents exiled by their government. In a statement issued by the office of the President's press spokesperson, the White House said the Soviet action violated recent understandings and was "an assault on the aspirations of all mankind to establish respect for human rights."

There appears to be little congressional enthusiasm for the proposed trade. "The Communists have broken the rules of the game time and time again," said one leading senator. "Of course, I have sympathy for the Kolokol family, but this is not the time for us to make any deal with the Soviets, especially if it involves returning convicted spies who can rework their way back into our intelligence community. It's time we taught the Kremlin we can play hard ball as well as the next guy."

We had not heard a word about Father. For all we knew, he was already in a work camp on the eastern frontier. His fate had been in the hands of others for fifteen months and would remain so for years to come. My fate was as yet undetermined, left for a large part to forces beyond my control. In a way, the trial was harder for Mother and me than for Father. Yes, he was the one sentenced to hard labor, but he at least knew what he now faced. Mother and I were left in the dark, alone, forced to deal with what all survivors must: the guilt, uncertainty, the remolding of a future without an important person. When the phone rang, we were the ones who heard, "You dirty traitorous scum! You're next. There is no room for troublemakers like you. We'll soon be rid of all of you!"

Even Yulia was not free from abuse. Already her playmates—no doubt on the instruction of their parents—were saying mean things or ignoring her. When we left the park, she was often in tears. "I don't want to go back tomorrow," she'd say. "I didn't do anything wrong. Father did."

"He didn't do anything wrong," I tried to explain. "He did what was right."

"Then why is he gone?"

I had no way to respond. "Come on, Yulia, Mother expects us home."

I, too, was subject to abuse. I found my locker at school broken into, my books torn, my sweater stolen. During gym I was repeatedly knocked down playing soccer, even when the ball was well downfield. None of the instructors intervened. I found obscene messages left on my chair. People "accidentally" spilled their soup on me during lunch.

Peter remained friendly. As I was sitting by myself in the lunchroom one afternoon, he came over and joined me. I trusted him less and less—but company was something that was scarce at school. "What are you going to do?" he asked.

"About what?" I said, keeping my eyes down at my food.

"What do you think the Americans are going to do?" he then asked.

"I don't know. How should I know?" I'd had my fill of questions.

"If they make the arrangements, would you leave Moscow?"

"It's up to my mother."

"Do you still hear from that Yakir girl?"

"Her name is Tanya. Tanya Yakir. No, not for months. We haven't gotten any personal mail, except for threats, since the trial."

137

"Is your mother going to release the report of your father's trial?"

I looked at Peter. "What report?"

"Come on, it's no secret. Everyone knows you made a record of the trial," he said. "I'm sure the authorities are well aware."

"So?"

"So . . . well, you're my friend, Lev. I don't want you to get into trouble," he said.

"And who told you there might be a record of the trial?"

"Oh, I don't remember," Peter said, obviously off guard. "Word gets around. Maybe you'd better cooperate and turn the record in before they search your place and find it. It's time for you to look out for yourself. Your mother can take care of herself."

"I don't know about any record of the trial," I said, getting up. "See you later, Peter."

Even without Malsa's notes from the first day, we were able to put together a detailed report of Father's trial. Our typewriter had been taken away, so we worked at Mochol's house. Late at night, when Mother and I left for home, Mochol would hide our notes behind the sink.

As we'd go down the stairs, Mochol's neighbors would open their doors to look at us. No one ever said anything, just stared for a moment before closing and locking their doors.

On the street, two agents would fall behind us and follow us home, occasionally stopping us at a busy intersection to harass us.

"What were you doing at Pevrod's apartment? Tell us, Citizen."

Mother would ignore the men, standing there only as long as it took the traffic to clear.

The night we finished the report, we didn't talk on the walk home as we usually did, discussing little episodes that had occurred at school or at the playground. Mother and Mochol had spent most of the evening trying to decide on our next move, under the noise of the radio. The authorities were waiting, it seemed, for either us or a Western nation to take the initiative.

"Someone must go to the West and appeal to the people themselves," Mochol said. "The governments aren't about to act without pressure."

"So one of us goes to the West and fails to raise public support, what then?" Mother asked. "The Soviets will never allow that person back in. Either way they win: either they get their spies back from America, or they're rid of another dissident. It's too risky."

"I should be the one to go, Irina," Mochol said. "I have nothing left to lose. They already took Lazar from me, what more could they want?"

"If anyone goes, it will be me," Mother said. "No offense, dear Mochol, but few Westerners know who you are, how important you really are. They know me. They know my face and know I am Sergei Ivanovich's wife. Besides, we need you here. I can't imagine how we would've made it without your bringing us extra food and money."

"You have done the same for me since Lazar was arrested," Mochol said, taking Mother's hand. "I can't imagine life without friends like you."

"What about me? Why can't I go?"

"Lev, the authorities would never let you leave. You're too young. Besides, I already know the network in the West; you don't. And it's important you're here with Grandma and Yulia."

"Other wives have left Russia with similar goals," I told her, "and their loved ones are still in prison."

139

"Would you rather we do nothing but wait for them to do as they wish?"

Mother and I walked briskly, trying to keep a distance between us and the agents.

"So you think the authorities will let you go?"

"Yes," she said, "I suspect they'll make it very easy. The problem will be if they won't let me return, if I fail to convince the Americans to release the Soviet spies."

"What could they do?"

"Any number of things, you know that. When I'm out of the country, they can label me a 'social parasite' or worse: Article 64 of the Criminal Code defines treason as 'flight abroad or refusal to return from abroad to the U.S.S.R.' While I'm in America, they could indict me for treason and I'll never be able to come back." The look she gave me told me she had already made up her mind to go. Neither I, nor Mochol, nor Grandma, nor Yulia would convince her otherwise. It was up to us only to approve and support her.

"And what will happen to us if you can't get back? What then?" I asked in an angry whisper.

"Mochol will watch over you. Grandma and you will take care of Yulia. Go to Mochol for anything; she is a survivor, she will help you to the end," she answered.

"To the end. That's wonderful," I laughed to myself.

"I know the Americans. They are a good people. I can't believe they will fail us. They have so little to give up— only the return of two spies. I know once I arrive and can meet with the political leaders, with the common people, I will make them understand. As a country that worships freedom above all, America will not desert us. But I have to act fast. Everything happens so fast in the West. We must get them to act before they forget us."

"Maybe the Americans have nothing to lose. Well, what about me? What about Yulia? How do you think we'll feel with both you and Father gone? Did you ever think we'd rather have you here, no matter what the circumstances are?"

"Yes, Lev. Yes. Yes." She took my arm. "But you saw Father at the trial. Do you think he can survive even a short prison term? I'm afraid they have broken his will to fight any longer. My trip is our only chance. I couldn't live with myself if I didn't go to America."

We walked the rest of the way home in silence. I couldn't put my thoughts together. I was exhausted, unable to counter Mother's stubborness with a logical alternative; I knew we had no alternative. She had to go. This made sense and it made me mad. I was angry with Mother, though I knew none of this was her fault. Neither, though, was it mine.

I felt the tension mount within me as we climbed the stairs to our apartment. One of our neighbors opened her door, checking on us as always. I could stand it no longer.

"Go to hell!" I yelled and punched the door as hard as I could, then grabbed the knob and slammed it shut.

"Lev!" Mother screamed, grabbing my arm and pulling me into our apartment. "What's wrong with you?"

I tried to sit down on the couch but slid to the floor. As if a plug had been pulled, the violence had released my anger, sadness, and frustration. I began to weep as I hadn't since childhood, unable to control my body's heaving. Ripples of pain and fear shook me, my physical self taking charge, releasing the emotions that had throttled my mind since Father's arrest. My eyesight blurred with tears, my throat gagged with mucus.

I heard Grandma rush from her room. "Irina, what's wrong with the boy?"

Mother waved her aside. "Let him be."

Then I said what I'd been holding in all this time, the one confession I feared might destroy what remained of my fragile family, "I miss Father!" I covered my face with my hands. "I hate him. I . . . I love him. I hate . . . all I know is I miss him."

Mother did not move. There was nothing she could do for me, anyway. "I know you do, Lev dear," she said quietly. "We all miss him."

I must have woken Yulia, for she appeared in the doorway, rubbing her eyes. "What's wrong with Lev?" she asked. "Mother, I'm frightened."

Slowly, I calmed myself. I knew nothing had changed, but at least I did feel relieved. "Nothing's wrong, Yulia. Go back to bed."

"Mother . . ."

"Grandma will see you to bed," Mother said. "I'll be in to kiss you in a moment."

"Come on, darling," Grandma whispered, taking Yulia's hand.

"Can I get you some tea?" Mother asked me.

"No, I'll be all right. Just give me a moment to catch my breath." I stayed on the floor, not yet knowing if I had enough control over my legs to stand. "Mother, did you know about Father and Malsa?"

"Yes," she said, going to the radio to turn it on, "almost from the beginning. It's hard to keep secrets in this house."

"So why did you stay with him?"

"Because I still loved him, and the work was important. There was a time your father and I adored each other, but the last couple of years it was mostly our work that kept us together. Your father is a great man, but he took advantage of Malsa, though she was more than willing, and he took advantage of me. You see, Lev, your father truly believed in what he was doing and often let his work get ahead of his loved ones. I know he needed me, but he rarely told me as much. Unlike Malsa, I devoted myself to the democratic movement for my own reasons, so my

142

conscience is clear: I am a decent woman. Father is a great man, this I know, but he's human, like the rest of us."

I leaned against the wall, my legs stretched in front of me. I studied my hands, for a moment wondering if they were mine.

"Lev, are you all right?" she asked after several minutes.

"Yes, at least I think so," I said, wiping my eyes and nose. I took several deep breaths. "I guess I needed that."

"I guess so," Mother said with a smile.

We sat there for perhaps five minutes. I felt very close to her, much more so in that silent time together than through all the words we had pushed toward each other in conversation. She was a good woman. She never lied to me, never hid the truth that life is more complicated than any of us care to imagine. I saw what Father saw in her: a strength deep in her being, an emotional resourcefulness that guided her through both tragedy and celebration.

I stood up, assured of my strength, and embraced her. "I love you, Mother."

"And I love you, dear son."

We hadn't taken the time to hold each other in the past months; there was too much to do and I suppose we lost sight of the importance of human contact, of physical reassurance. As with Tanya, I don't think of that embrace as one of goodbye; rather, as one in honor of the eternal mystery of love and remembrance.

18

MISSION FROM MOSCOW

by Percy Elliman

Irina Kolokol, the wife of the jailed Soviet dissident Sergei Ivanovich Kolokol, is on a tour of the United States. She held a press conference today in which she spoke of her husband's plight and her hope for an international arrangement which would free him.

This is Mrs. Kolokol's first visit outside the Soviet Union. "I'm amazed at the diversity one sees on the streets. The openness. It is not like this in Moscow," she said. "Casual dress and behavior, and so much freedom of expression. I watched the television news last night in the hotel. It was critical of both your political leaders and their opponents. I don't think all Americans realize that no one in Russia is allowed such a luxury."

At the time of Sergei Ivanovich Kolokol's conviction of "anti-Soviet propaganda and agitation" it was generally believed by his supporters in the West that the

United States was prepared to exchange two convicted Soviet spies for Mr. Kolokol's freedom. However, in the ensuing weeks, neither the White House nor the Kremlin has confirmed such an arrangement. Mrs. Kolokol, at the risk of not being allowed to return to her family, left Moscow to appeal personally to the Congress and the American people to pressure the White House to propose the trade.

"The admirable characteristic about the West," Mrs. Kolokol said, "is its long tradition of democracy and liberty dating back hundreds of years, from the Magna Carta to the American and French revolutions, even encompassing the recent hippie and anti-war movements. The Russian people have no such tradition. We can be the kindest, most generous people in the world, but we have always had to live under authoritarian regimes. This is one reason it is so hard to rally support for democratic ideals within the Soviet Union. People there are not used to freedom—perhaps it scares them. So we are dependent on the Western nations to keep our movement from being wiped out by the state."

Many groups involved in human-rights issues are sponsoring Mrs. Kolokol's tour. The groups working for Sergei Ivanovich Kolokol's release range from international organizations involved in issues of intellectual and religious freedom to small neighborhood committees writing letters and collecting petitions across the nation.

"It is important my husband's release is obtained before too much time passes and people forget him," Mrs. Kolokol responded when asked about the timing of her visit. "Sergei Ivanovich is a symbol, both to people of conscience worldwide and to the Kremlin. By working for his freedom, for the freedom of all people imprisoned solely for their work in the human-rights area, the West will be sending a message to the Soviet leadership, to tyrants everywhere, that violations of recent agreements assuring loosening of restrictions of free travel and censorship will not be tolerated."

After meeting with the mayor and city council, Mrs. Kolokol will address a rally in downtown Manhattan tomorrow.

Then she's scheduled to appear in other major cities —Philadelphia, Miami, Chicago, St. Louis, Los Angeles —before meeting the President at a White House reception.

145

I read over several times the article Mochol had brought us, trying to get a sense of how Mother's journey was going. It seemed to be off to a good start. It was still impossible to predict if she would be successful or not. Even the authorities here did not know how it would turn out, so they basically left us alone, harassing us no more than we'd grown accustomed to. They were waiting, too.

Since nothing would be resolved for several weeks, I decided it was safe to accompany my class on a special trip. The school had arranged for a showing of a new movie at the October Cinema, a large movie house near the Central Post Office.

Like everything that reaches the public—books, magazines, announcements, posters—the movie was made and approved by the Soviets. It turned out to be one of the rash of recent films dealing with the Great Patriotic War, or World War II. The film carried a most peculiar and disturbing message, for it depicted wealthy Jews as being responsible for Hitler's rise to power and his attack on Russia. It went so far as to show wealthy Jews ordering the Nazis to exterminate the middle-class and poor Jews so the wealthy ones could take the dead Jews' possessions. I knew this was a vicious lie, since I had read about the war in books from my parents' library. But what about my classmates? Would they believe this "history" the Soviets were creating as part of their campaign against the Jews? Could they possibly discern truth from propaganda?

When I got home, Grandma handed me a letter Mochol had been given by Simon Reese. It was a letter from America, flown to Moscow in the diplomatic pouch. I opened the envelope, turned up the radio, and read aloud:

Dearest Lev, Yulia, and Grandma:

I fear to report my trip is not as we hoped. Everyone here has been nice to me, but the general public does not seem concerned for Father.

Last night I spoke to a small group at a church in St. Louis. It was supposed to be an important event, attended by the local congressman and other officials.

When the congressman arrived, we had our photograph taken together. He was pleasant but formal, talking mainly about the Cardinals of St. Louis—whatever they may be. We sat on a stage, and when I was introduced by my local hostess, the audience applauded me. There were about one hundred people there.

The congressman spoke first and gave a short speech. He talked about how important it was to demonstrate to the Soviets that the United States is a strong, powerful country. He reminded the audience how he had voted for every new military program over the past two years. He asked for their votes—he called their votes "support" —since his reelection was coming up soon. As he spoke I noticed his aide looking at her watch and checking a schedule. The aide was nervous and motioned to the congressman to hurry. When the congressman finished, calling our conversation "worthwhile and fruitful," he left the church. I was told he was due to give a different speech at a union hall in ten minutes.

When I spoke I noticed a woman in the audience knitting. A man was napping. Others were talking among themselves. Some people even got up and left before I finished. I did my best. I told them how important their active support is. I said the fighters for human rights around the world must know they are not alone, that there are many people fighting with them, sharing the struggle. But I feel no one was listening. It was so frustrating.

Afterward I answered questions. People asked what they could do and I told them to write letters to their leaders to pressure the Soviets. I told them pressure from the free nations was our best hope. Most of the questions showed me how little most Americans know or care about other parts of the world.

147

The next morning the local newspaper carried a story about my speech, but most of the article concerned the congressman's comments on national defense. It even had his picture—I was cut out.

I still have hopes that the President will listen to me. I hear he is a man of principle, though some people tell me he will do only what makes sense for his political future. I can't believe fighting for Father's release could do anything but help the President.

I miss you terribly. America is an exciting place, but it is not home.

With all my love,
Mother

P.S.   Tanya sends her love to all.

A week passed before we received another letter from Mother. During this time I came home from school one afternoon to find two KGB agents waiting inside our apartment. I can't say I was surprised to see them. It gave me an indication that the authorities were growing impatient with the inability of the Americans to formally propose a trade. The Soviets wanted an end to our story.

"What do you want?" I asked the agents.

"Sit down, Lev Kolokol," one of them said. "We know you are hiding a transcript of your father's trial record, and we will find it."

So, as they had done before, the agents started to go through our possessions. They did not leave for hours, and when they did they had to back up a van to load everything they confiscated. They took all our books— saying the official censors must go through them to make certain they were not anti-Soviet. They took our radio— to prevent us from listening to "foreign propaganda and lies." Boxes of personal letters were taken on suspicion that they contained names of other dissidents and foreign agents. Any sharp objects—including our silverware and

148

my razor—were removed for "our own protection," as if they cared if we slit our own throats.

The house was suddenly barren. A house empty of personal things is alien. They would do what they could to dehumanize us, to make us non-persons.

That night Mochol came over with a roast she had received from the food shop in exchange for doing the clerk's laundry. She looked at our empty bookcases.

"Those animals," she whispered. She went into the kitchen and put the roast in the oven.

I followed her. "Mochol—"

"Lev, shhh!" She motioned me to her and whispered, "It's no longer safe to speak here. We'll go for a walk."

Outside, Mochol and I headed for the park, hoping the agents wouldn't be overly suspicious of us.

"Is the trial record still safe?" I whispered.

"Yes, but I don't know for how much longer. I have to think my apartment is next to be ransacked. For all we know, they're there now, tearing up the floorboards."

A car slowed down near us. Inside, I could see four men. The windows were down; a lit cigarette glowed from the front seat.

Mochol took my arm and guided me toward the storefronts, away from the street. "We must act as soon as possible, Lev. I suspect their next step is to drag you before Akakievich and threaten you with arrest. I think we should get the trial record to Simon Reese as soon as possible. If they won't release Sergei Ivanovich, at least the world will know what a sham his trial was."

"How long does it take to make a microfilm copy?"

"I know people who can do it overnight. Why?"

"Mochol, this may sound stupid, but I want to tell my story, our story, not just release the trial record. Without the context of our lives, I don't know if anyone will truly understand what happened at the trial."

"Lev, you don't have much time—a week at the most."

"It's important, Mochol. It's important my parents know, the Kremlin knows, that I stood up. Father had his life's work to mark his dedication; I have my life to mark my conscience."

"Well, we'll stop by my apartment. I'll give you some paper. Make certain you wrap it around your thighs so the agents can't spot it." She stopped me, making certain I'd hear her. "One week, Lev, that's all you have. If your writing isn't done by then, I'll go ahead and release the trial record. Understand?"

"Yes." Already I was mapping out in my mind what I wanted to recount.

Six days later, Mochol brought over Mother's letter.

"Simon Reese reports the news is bad," she whispered. "He's heard from Washington."

"What? The trade is off?"

"Shhh," she whispered. "Read, don't talk."

Dear Lev, Yulia, and Grandma:

I am writing from Washington, D.C. This was the day I hoped to meet the President of the United States, to stand at his side while he announced the arrangements for Father's freedom.

Washington is an elegant city, the closest city America has to Leningrad. There are many parks and marble buildings. One does not see many people, but the streets are busy with cars and buses.

This morning I took a long walk along the Potomac River. I'm told George Washington's house is up the river, but I won't have time to visit it.

Everyone in Washington talks about the government, but mostly all they share is the latest gossip: what official is involved in a scandal, who is likely to lose an election, who is invited to use the White House tennis courts, who is sleeping with whom, which important person has a drinking problem.

I never met the President. Instead, I met one of his many aides, who told me the President was very busy and would try to call me later. He never did, but his wife reached me at the hotel. She asked me if I had seen the lovely flowers planted beside the White House. The aide told me the President was doing all he could to help Father. But I no longer believe this.

Percy told me the President decided it was "bad for his image" to make a deal with the Kremlin. The American public is currently supporting increased military spending. They are afraid the Soviets now have the edge. Every night on the television some "expert" reports how a military build-up should be the first priority for the country. So they are willing to forget us for the time being.

I don't know what the future holds. I am trying to prepare myself, knowing I will not see you for a long time, but this fact is impossible for me to accept. I will continue to work for our family, this is all I can say. I know the Soviets and that they will never let me return home. Still, I work and hope for good news that one day we shall all be free at last. Keep good faith. I miss you terribly.

I don't know what else to write at this time.

Love,
Mother

The next day, Mochol brought the newspaper. There in print was the confirmation of what I had already accepted as fact.

FREEDOM SWITCH FIZZLES:
SPOUSE STRANDED STATESIDE
by Percy Elliman

Blaming the lack of public support, an influential White House insider said that any deal to free Soviet dissenter S. I. Kolokol was "on the back burner, a low priority."

"Considering the President's public position toward the Soviets, we just can't take a chance, even though we feel sympathy for the plight of the Kolokol family and

151

those who fight for human rights around the world," the official added.

Although human rights are supposedly a consideration in all foreign affairs, the White House does not believe the public is sufficiently attracted to the Kolokol case to merit the political fallout.

When asked if political considerations were the criteria in stating a trade could be made and then deciding not to pursue Kolokol's release, the White House official responded sharply, "Of course not! The Administration is committed to the importance of human dignity. However, our perception is that the American public would rather see our energies directed toward increasing our military strength in order that we can approach the other side about mutual arms reduction. In the long run, we believe our policy will increase Soviet respect for the rights of its citizens."

S. I. Kolokol's wife, Irina, is apparently stranded in this country, since the Soviets will not allow her to return to Moscow. Whether the Kremlin counted on the American reaction to rid themselves of one of their best-known critics can only be suspected.

There has been no word about the fate of S. I. Kolokol since his trial ended some weeks ago. It is assumed he is serving the harsh sentence handed down by the Soviet tribunal.

That night Grandma and I laid out our warmest clothes, not knowing if we'd be sent away to the eastern frontier. My writing was nearly completed, ready to put with the account of Father's trial. I didn't know if I would be allowed to finish it. I thought about destroying it all, not allowing it to end up in some court file. Was I crazy to be doing this? No, I decided I could not leave my story unfinished, but told Grandma if ever I was late coming home to burn it without a second thought.

The agents came the next morning—not to send us away, not to turn over our furniture and rip open our mattresses. No, this time they were almost polite.

"Lev Kolokol, you are requested to appear at the Procurator's Office immediately. Please come with us."

"How long will this take?" I asked.

"Don't ask questions, just find your coat. You should be home for supper," one of the agents told me.

I looked at Grandma. She nodded slightly, letting me know she would wait until dark before destroying my story.

19

"Sorry to keep you waiting, young Kolo-kol," Akakievich said, entering his office. He sat down at his desk and glanced over some papers, then looked at me with a tilt of his head. "This must be a difficult time, what with your parents gone. Are you getting along?"

"As if you care," I responded coldly.

Akakievich shook his head, "Such cynicism in someone so young! Events can still work out in your favor. All you have to do is cooperate with us and you will be surprised how easy life shall be for you in the future."

I didn't respond. I knew Akakievich would first try to "reason" with me, perhaps offer me an "arrangement" by which he would receive the trial record and I'd be allowed to retain my "freedom."

"I understand how you feel, Lev," he said, softening his tone, "for I have a son your age. Growing up is not an easy thing. My son has his problems. He's not as good a student as you—though I see your grades have been disappointing of late—but he's learning how to make the best of life. He's a good boy, even if he's not too bright, and he's determined to take advantage of what our great system has to offer and hopes to have a career in the military. He's learned to follow authority—an important lesson. I'm proud of him."

I remained silent. What did I care about his son?

"Perhaps you wonder why I asked to see you," Akakievich said, standing up and walking around his desk to sit near me. "Well, I'm concerned about you. I remember our first meeting. You impressed me then. And of course I saw you at your father's trial. Again I felt for your situation. It's none of your doing you were born into the wrong family. If you'll let me, I'd like to help you."

I pushed my chair back to increase the distance between us. "Why should I trust you?"

"I can appreciate your suspicions. You have no reason to believe me," he said. "If I were in your position, I'd probably feel the same way. I admire your intelligence— you're nobody's fool. So tell me, how are things going?"

"All you have to do is read your reports," I said, pointing to the papers on his desk. "I'm sure you have files on everything I do. You know how I'm treated at school. You know that my home is still watched day and night, even with my parents gone. What could I possibly hide from the state?"

Akakievich smiled. "Your parents have taught you well. You are definitely the son of Sergei and Irina Kolokol. But you've learned to be suspicious of even the best intentions. Your parents did wrong and now must suffer the consequences. I was only doing my job to prosecute the enemies of our people. But you, Lev, you've done nothing wrong. I'm not out to get you. I don't want to see you sent away. You're still a young man with a long, productive future before you. I didn't have to see you this morning. I'm a busy man and have more pressing matters I should attend to. Won't you let me help?"

"May I leave now?" I said. "I'm late for class."

As if on cue, his expression changed. He stood up and moved behind his desk. He picked up his telephone and asked an aide to come in. "Suit yourself, young Kolokol. I was hoping we could work things out like two gentlemen, but perhaps I overestimated your maturity. I did not want to be harsh, but your attitude leaves me little choice."

The aide entered, carrying a folder which he handed to Akakievich; then he stationed himself by the door. Akakievich opened the folder.

"We know you and your mother made a record of your father's trial," he said. "This is an illegal act. The court has sole possession of all material concerning any proceeding. We want that record. You will turn it over voluntarily or we'll be forced to consider stronger measures to obtain it. Don't think you can play with us."

"I don't know what you're talking about," I said. "Your agents thoroughly searched our home. If there was a record of Father's trial I'm sure they would have found it."

"Don't get smart with me, Citizen Kolokol," Akakievich said, raising his voice. "I don't have time for childish antics. Will you turn the record over? I demand an answer!"

"I'd like to cooperate, but I have no record," I said.

"Is this your statement?"

"Yes. I have no such record."

"So be it. You will not leave this office until I return.

156

Perhaps the time to reflect will make you see the danger-ous direction you are taking." With that, Akakievich stood up and quickly left, leaving the aide to watch me.

Again, the waiting game.

I had learned patience. There was a time when Akakie-vich's tactics might have worked, reducing me to tears. But I had grown strong, hard. I no longer chewed at my fingernails until I tore the skin. I would not be intimi-dated. They had nothing on me.

When Akakievich returned, after nearly an hour, he was carrying a black plastic bag with a tag around its neck. He placed the bag on his desk and sat down.

"So have you changed your mind?" he asked.

I did not say anything.

"Why make my job difficult? Do you think I want to see you suffer more anguish? Can't you act like a man, a proper citizen, and cooperate?"

I looked around the room, then shrugged my shoulders.

"Very well." Akakievich untied the bag and reached inside, bringing out the magazine Percy had given me, the one the KGB agents had taken when they searched my room. Akakievich leafed through the pages, stopping to look at the pictures, shaking his head. "It is a very serious crime to be in possession of pornographic material, Citizen Kolokol. This is yours, isn't it?"

Again I said nothing. I was surprised, but far from shocked, that the magazine had been turned over to Akakievich.

"This was found in your room, and I should make certain you suffer the legal punishment for possession. Of course, I may be willing to overlook this infraction if you give us the record of your father's trial. Try to under-stand, if you release this record to the West it will only be used to embarrass our leadership. Foreigners will do with the record what they wish, change it for their own purposes. They will use you, exploit the facts for their own propaganda. You will gain nothing by the record's release."

"I don't have any record," I said.

"So you say." Akakievich reached into the bag again, this time removing an envelope, which he opened. It contained the paper on which Peter had written the formula for making gunpowder. "I'm not a chemist by training," Akakievich said, "but I know a recipe for making contraband material when I see it. If I'm not mistaken, this is a formula for making powerful bombs, is this correct?"

"I wouldn't know."

"You wouldn't, would you? This, too, was found in a search of your room. My suspicions are you were planning to use this formula to anti-Soviet ends. Is this correct?"

"It's only a chemistry formula," I tried. to explain. "I needed it for school. Why would I make a bomb?"

"Because you are the bitter, misguided son of two social misfits," Akakievich said in a stern voice. "Because you want to see our glorious Soviet system destroyed and will go to any means to see this happen. Because the same treasonous blood that flows in your parents' veins flows in yours. Because you have delusions of becoming a martyr, never to be forgotten, by planting a bomb that will kill innocent citizens." He smashed his fist down on his desk. "I'm tired of treating you like a sensible person. Either you turn over the trial record or I will see you suffer the same fate as your father. We have no pity for the likes of you."

"I . . . I . . ."

"Don't lie to me again, Kolokol! I won't stand for it!"

"I . . ." My voice wavered. I tried to control myself, not wanting to break down in front of Akakievich. "I haven't done anything wrong," I tried to explain. "And what makes you think I'd be so stupid as to use that

158

formula to actually make explosives? What proof do you have?"

"Proof? You want proof?" Akakievich shouted. "I want an answer! Now! Will you hand over the trial record?"

"I said I don't have it."

"Quiet! I've had my fill of you." He leaned back in his chair, trying to break me with his silent stare.

I said nothing, keeping my eyes away from him.

He reached into the bag one last time and removed something that I had nearly forgotten about. It was Georgy's old coat, the one I gave to Peter the day we set off the explosives in the field. "Do you recognize this? Of course you do," he said, not giving me a chance to respond. "This is your coat, isn't it? Of course it is."

"Where did you get that?"

"Let's say a loyal young man knew it was his duty, his honor, to turn it over to the proper authorities."

"So?"

"So do you admit this is your coat?"

"What if it is my coat? So what? I gave it to a friend—a schoolmate of mine—when he tore his clothing. It was a cold day. We were playing in a field. He was shivering. What difference does a silly coat make, anyway?"

"This coat has been analyzed in our lab. There are powder burns on one sleeve. Powder burns, I am told, from a very powerful explosion. We suspect you were wearing this when setting off a bomb. There has been a series of unsolved bombings in Moscow over the past year. And we now have every reason—and evidence—to believe you set them off. This is a serious charge, Citizen, one that will result in a long sentence in a work camp. Unless . . ."

"Unless what?" I said.

"Unless you cooperate fully and turn over what you still possess: an illegal record of your father's trial. We want to close the door on the sad episode of your parents' anti-

Soviet activities. We want this disgusting chapter forgotten."

I sighed deeply. So Tanya was right after all. Peter had chosen to subvert our friendship. His loyalty was to his family, to the Party, rather than to me; this wasn't surprising. I believe Peter was convinced he was doing the right thing to turn me in—it was impossible for him to think any other way, even if one day he might feel guilty for betraying a friend. In the end he was no better than my classmates who ignored me. In one way he was much worse; at least they'd been honest in their contempt for me. Peter hadn't.

I looked up at Akakievich and shook my head.

"Now you know where we stand," he said, coming around the desk, acting friendly as he did before. "We shall use this evidence against you if we have to. We shall send you away if you force us to. It's up to you. You have two options—and only two. Either you remain stubborn and suffer the severe consequences of your insolence. Or . . ." He looked at me.

I suppose I was to finish his sentence; instead I repeated, "Or?"

"Or you cooperate. We have the power to make your life a joy to live. We can help you achieve professional status. We could make certain you, your grandmother, and your sister are well provided for."

"So all I'd have to do is turn in the record and you'll leave us alone?"

"We could do more than simply leave you alone. I am certain we could arrange for your family to join your mother in America. How about that? Remember, we don't have to do a damn thing for you. But I'm trying to do what's best. I have children of my own."

"How am I to trust you? How do I know you'll keep your word if I turn in the trial record?"

Akakievich turned his hands palms up. "What choice

160

do you have? Wouldn't you rather join your mother and your girl friend—oh, yes, I know all about you and Tanya Yakir—in America than face conviction here? Can your personal conscience be so high that you'd sacrifice your family life for what peace of mind you might have in a labor camp? Come on, Lev, be reasonable."

"I'll do the right thing. Don't worry." I knew then that there really was only one thing to do if I ever was to live with myself. Akakievich had convinced me of the right course of action.

"Good," he said. "You can go now. My aide will drive you home to get the transcript and then to school to explain to the principal why you were detained. Everything will be taken care of."

"Comrade Akakievich, my decision won't just affect me. My sister and Grandma are concerned. My grandma is an old woman, set in her ways. If she's forced to leave Moscow, she'll make quite a scene. I know this. Can I have tonight to talk to her, to convince her the best thing is for us to join Mother in America? That Father's case is not for us to resolve, but better left to the authorities? I can appreciate that you want to end this quietly. So do I. I've had my fill of tension, of reporters asking questions, of uncertainty. I'd like to leave as quietly as possible. But without Grandma's cooperation, I'm afraid she might create a terrible stir when we arrive in America." I looked at him, hoping he would understand. "One night, Comrade Akakievich, that's all I'm asking for."

He started to speak, "No, I can't—"

"One night! What difference will one night make after all these months? Please, on my honor, grant me a chance to convince my grandma to cooperate."

"Tomorrow morning. Same time. No further delay will be tolerated." He turned to the aide and nodded his head. "Drive him to school and make certain he enters the building." Then to me: "Tomorrow. Ten o'clock."

20

At school I saw Peter during gym. The class was divided into two teams for water polo. Peter and I were on opposite sides.

We were treading water in the deep end, away from the ball, which was at the other end of the pool.

"You were late," Peter said, already winded. "Why?"

"I had to go somewhere."

"News of your father? Your mother?"

I looked down the pool. One of Peter's teammates had stolen the ball and was turning toward the goal I was defending. The ball was thrown on the fly, landing between Peter and me.

He started to move for the ball, then stopped, waiting for me to make a move.

"What are you waiting for?" I asked. "Go after it."

"Lev, I . . . I want to explain."

"What's there to explain? It's only a game, right? Make your move, you little bastard!"

Peter took a quick stroke and reached the ball, cradling it with his free arm. He pivoted, positioning himself for a shot at my goal. Lifting the ball out of the water, he cocked his arm. He was no more than a meter from me.

I squeezed my legs together and leaped on top of him, pushing him under the water. The ball slid away. I had my hands on his shoulders, forcing him down, kneeing him in the chest. He was trying to grab my legs, climb up my body to the surface. But I held him under until the instructor blew his whistle.

"Kolokol, that's enough. Let him go."

I released Peter. He thrashed to the surface, coughing, staring at me.

"Good, Kolokol. That's the type of aggressive play I want to see from all of you," the instructor said. "That's the stuff champions are made of."

I shook the water from my hair.

On my way home from school I stopped by the Central Post Office to make a phone call. I dialed the number. "Yes," a voice on the other end of the line answered.

"This is Lev Kolokol. I've seen an official at the office. I want to set up an appointment."

"Just a moment. I'll put your call through."

I looked out the booth at the illuminated globe revolving in the middle of the lobby. A group of children surrounded it, accompanied by their teacher, who was pointing at various spots on the world with a wooden pole. The globe turned, no matter who watched it, and I remembered the times I had visited it with my family. Once I followed the red star that marked Moscow's location in its orbit. I had to walk fast, since the globe turned at a

163

moderate speed. Now another group of children gathered to watch the world turn.

"Yes," a familiar voice in the telephone said. "I believe we can help. I've been expecting your call."

"I thought so," I said.

"Don't worry. When will you be ready?"

"It must be tomorrow morning," I said.

"No problem. We'll have someone meet you near the water, away from the wall, at nine-thirty. She'll be wearing something to protect her from the cold and carrying something you'll recognize."

"And then?" I asked.

"We'll take care of the arrangements. Don't worry."

"Good," I said, hanging up.

Leaving the Post Office, I was followed to Mochol Pevrod's. The agents kept their distance, perhaps on instructions from Akakievich not to harass me.

When Mochol opened the door, she quickly motioned me inside and turned on her radio.

"Lev, I was worried about you." She hugged me. "I took food to your apartment and your grandma said they had sent for you. What about your father's trial record? Your story?"

I shook my head. "They have to go out tomorrow morning. Akakievich thinks I'm talking Grandma into leaving for America in exchange for the record. I have only till ten o'clock tomorrow, when I'm due back in his office. Can you get the manuscript microfilmed tonight?"

"If we must, we must." She shrugged. "But what about your story? Is it finished?"

"No." Then I remembered telling Grandma to destroy my manuscript if I was late getting home. "Mochol, the rest of my writing is at home. Can you go get it and tell Grandma I'm here?"

"Of course," she said. "I'll hide it under my skirt. With hips like mine, the agents won't notice I'm hiding something." She went to her desk. "Here is some paper and a pen. I should be back within an hour."

So I sat at Mochol's table, not taking time to correct my mistakes, and wrote out the last sections of my story.

When she returned, Mochol bothered me only to put a glass of tea at my side. I took a break, shaking my hand, trying to loosen the cramp from my fingers. My neck hurt from craning over the table.

"What about tomorrow?" she asked.

"I called Simon Reese from the Post Office," I told her. "He'll have someone meet me on the way to Akakievich's. Watch over Yulia and Grandma."

"You know I will," she said.

The memory of the day's meeting with Akakievich was fresh, so I had no trouble re-creating it. I brought my story up to the very moment I was writing, then stopped. But this was no way to end.

I have no way of knowing how my story will end; no one holds the future that squarely in sight. But there are times, brief moments of intuition about how events will work out. Predicting the future is not a rational process; it is based on mere feelings, on a sense of how time will unfold and what actions seem destined to intercede.

I feel the need to complete this long episode of my life, to bring it to a close, an understanding, so I can look to my future.

There are great ebbs and flows in how a society and its individuals function, and thus evolves the character of a people. It's a strange process, the exchange of power from the masses to the top, and then back again: that a people may finally reject the manner by which it was led.

I look at my fellow citizens, under the firm control of the Soviet system, and can expect no revolutionary change. Still, there are my parents and others like me— people committed to the hope of a free society. Under the harshest treatment—in nearly all parts of the world—

this hope has never been extinguished. Tyrants and repression have come and gone and the spiritual sense of how we can lead good decent lives remains. If the times demand it, those who struggle for human rights will go underground, only to emerge stronger for the hardships they have suffered. Freedom and dignity are so integral a part of the human condition that no system of oppression will ever successfully erase them.

It has not been an easy life; but it is mine. I have lived it freely, becoming, I hope, a better, kinder person in the process.

So I now create an end to this story, knowing well I shall be punished severely for my disloyalty to the Soviet authority. But there must be a higher authority than any reigning government. My conscience, my being, cannot act any other way.

Early tomorrow morning Mochol will come to our apartment with a chicken she exchanged for some pears she canned last autumn.

The agents across the street stop and harass her, looking through her bag, making her empty her pockets. Not finding anything suspicious, they let her go.

She brings the chicken into the kitchen and unwraps it. She puts a finger to her lips, indicating I shouldn't talk.

"Now, Lev, have Grandma just heat this up later for tonight's dinner. I already stuffed and cooked it at home. Here, taste the stuffing." She reaches inside the chicken and removes several tiny spools of microfilm wrapped in plastic: my story, small enough to fit in the palm of my hand.

I kiss Mochol on both cheeks. "It looks delicious!"

After Mochol leaves, I wait awhile before going outside. As I close the front door and enter the street, a soft snow begins to fall. An early autumn reminder of winter's inevitability.

I quickly fall in among the Muscovites on their way to work, crowding the sidewalks. It is nine o'clock. I have sixty minutes to arrive at Akakievich's office. I walk fast, making certain to stay among the crowd, hoping to lose the agents following me.

By the time I reach the center of Moscow, the snow has left a thin cover on the ground. The sky is gray, the sun blocked by clouds, but the weather has a strange insulating effect, layering all buildings with a clean white skin.

I turn into Red Square, and walk the length of the square, toward its lower corner along the Moskva River, and stop near the Cathedral of the Intercession. The cathedral is the oldest building in Red Square, built in the sixteenth century at the orders of Ivan the Terrible. It is a sight familiar to all Muscovites and therefore largely ignored, left to the tourists to pose in front of.

There I see her, in a large group of tourists. A small thin camera in one hand, a red scarf wrapped around her neck. She is middle-aged, perhaps Mother's age; her clothes identify her as a foreigner, for her fur coat is thick and glossy. When I approach, I see in her other hand a book, Yeats's *Collected Poems*, that my parents had read aloud from on many evenings. She moves to the center of the group, as if she wants to hear the tourist guide's description more clearly. I follow her so that we are both surrounded by the group.

I reach into my pocket, and when we touch hands I pass the microfilm to her. We say nothing. She puts the microfilm in her pocket, and then takes out something that she hands to me. She smiles, and walks away from the group. When I last see her, she is aiming her camera at the cathedral.

167

I look at what she has given me. It is a strip of four photographs, a sequence of Tanya slowly breaking, from top to bottom, into a wide smile. She looks so pretty, her hair cut in layers like a movie star's.

On the back of the strip is this message: "I won my first gymnastic meet here. Not bad, huh? I love you and think of you all the time! We will not say it shall not be. You've made everyone so proud. Kisses. Tanya."

Seeing her again makes me happy, her face so full of life. I open my coat and put the strip into my chest pocket.

My life is before me. I turn and walk away from the Kremlin walls, toward home.